WAR,
RACISM
AND
ECONOMIC INJUSTICE
The Global Ravages of Capitalism

FIDEL CASTRO

Edited by Alexandra Keeble

Published in association with Editora Politica, Havana

OCEAN PRESS
Melbourne • New York

www.oceanbooks.com.au

Cover design by David Spratt

ISBN 1-876175-47-8

First printed 2002

Printed in Australia

Library of Congress Control Number: 2001095068

Published by Ocean Press
Australia: GPO Box 3279, Melbourne, Victoria 3001, Australia
        ●Fax: (61-3) 9329 5040   ●E-mail: info@oceanbooks.com.au
USA: PO Box 1186 Old Chelsea Station, New York, NY 10113-1186, USA

OCEAN PRESS DISTRIBUTORS
United States and Canada: LPC Group,
        1436 West Randolph St, Chicago, IL 60607, USA
Britain and Europe: Global Book Marketing,
        38 King Street, London, WC2E 8JT, UK
Australia and New Zealand: Astam Books,
        57-61 John Street, Leichhardt, NSW 2040, Australia
Cuba and Latin America: Ocean Press,
        Calle 21 #406, Vedado, Havana, Cuba

www.oceanbooks.com.au

CONTENTS

1. Interview with Federico Mayor Zaragoza, former UNESCO Director General, January 24, 2000   **1**

2. Address to the Millennium Summit of the United Nations, New York, September 6, 2000   **23**

3. The Tragedy of AIDS in the Third World, UN Millennium Summit, New York, September 7, 2000   **27**

4. The Role of the United Nations in the 21st Century, UN Millennium Summit, New York, September 7, 2000   **31**

5. Riverside Church, Harlem, September 8, 2000   **37**

6. National Assembly, Caracas, Venezuela, October 27, 2000   **61**

7. The 10th Ibero-American Summit, Panama City, November 17 & 18, 2000   **73**

8. On History and Humanity, Public Forum, Havana Province, January 27, 2001   **79**

9. Message to Protestors at the Quebec "Free Trade Area of the Americas" Summit, April 17, 2001   **85**

10. Inter-Parliamentary Union, Havana, April 5, 2001   **87**

11. The Trial of General Augusto Pinochet for War Crimes, April 28, 2001   **95**

12. On Globalization and Latin America, Havana, May 1, 2001   **99**

13. World Conference against Racism, Racial Discrimination, Xenophobia and Related Intolerance, Durban, South Africa, September 1, 2001   **107**

14. The U.S. "War on Terrorism," Havana, September 22, 2001   **113**

15. On the Present Economic and World Crisis, Havana, November 2, 2001   **119**

Editor's Note

This book is a sharp, brief selection of recent speeches and interviews with Fidel Castro, dating from June 2000 to November 2001. Among them are speeches given in Venezuela, Panama, Cuba, the United States and South Africa. Also included are interventions to the Millennium Summit held at the United Nations in 2000 and a landmark speech to the Racism Conference held in Durban, South Africa, in August 2001.

Here, the Cuban leader presents a damning indictment of the present world economic and political order. In these dark times of media manipulation and U.S. hegemony, Fidel Castro's is a voice from the Third World that very much needs to circulated. Special note must be made of the final two items in this selection, speeches given by Fidel Castro on September 22 and November 2, 2001, in which he calls on the world to unite against both terrorism and war — a cry for justice and peace in the face of the September 11, 2001 terrorist attacks in the United States, as well as the war against Afghanistan that was about to erupt. They are somber notes on which to conclude, but no less challenging than the overall content of this book, which calls for fundamental transformation of the world economic and social order.

This book is published in association with Editora Politica of Havana. The director of Editora Politica, Santiago Dorques, provided support and encouragement for the project. This book is the continuation of a previous editorial project published in 2000 as *Capitalism in Crisis — Globalization and World Politics Today,* also by Fidel Castro. Readers of this book are urged to consult the volume that preceded it.

Finally, the website of Ocean Press provides a valuable resource for those seeking to challenge the world order and to fight for global and social justice. It truly is as the home page announces: *Ideas for radical change*, and is worth visiting at **www.oceanbooks.com.au**

Alex Keeble
November 2001

1

"People used to talk about apartheid in South Africa. Today we could talk about apartheid throughout the world, where over four billion human beings are deprived of the most basic rights."

Interview with Federico Mayor Zaragoza, former UNESCO Director General
January 24, 2000

Federico Mayor — *With China, Vietnam and North Korea, Cuba is considered the last bulwark of socialism. Ten years after the fall of the Berlin Wall, does the word "socialism" make sense any more?*

Fidel Castro — Today I am more convinced than ever that it makes a great deal of sense. What happened 10 years ago was the naïve and unwitting destruction of a great social historical process, that needed to be improved, but not destroyed. Its destruction was not even achieved by Hitler's hordes, though they killed over 20 million Soviets and devastated half of the country. Ten years ago, the world was left under the aegis of a single superpower, which did not contribute even five percent of the sacrifices made by the Soviets in the fight against fascism.

In Cuba, we have a united country and a party that guides but does not nominate or elect. The people, gathered in public assemblies, nominate candidates, and elect delegates from 14,686 districts. This is the foundation of our electoral system. The delegates make up the assemblies of their respective municipalities and nominate candidates to the provincial and national assemblies — the highest bodies of state power at those levels. The delegates, who are chosen through a secret ballot, must receive over 50 percent of the valid votes in their corresponding jurisdictions.

Although voting is not compulsory, over 95 percent of eligible voters take part in these elections. Many people in the world have not bothered to look at these facts.

The United States, such a vocal advocate of multiparty systems, has two parties that are so perfectly similar in their methods, objectives and goals that they have practically created the most perfect one-party system in the world. Over 50 percent of the people in that "democratic country" do not even cast a vote, and the team that manages to raise the most funds often wins, with the votes of only 25 percent of the electorate. The political system is undermined by disputes, vanity and personal ambition or by interest groups operating within the established economic and social model, and there is no real alternative for a change in the system.

When the small English-speaking nations of the Caribbean achieved independence, they put into place more efficient parliamentary systems where the ruling party remains in power as long as it enjoys consensus. These are much more stable than the presidential regimes imposed on the rest of Latin America, which have copied the U.S. model.

Under capitalism, it is the large national and international companies that actually govern, even in the most highly industrialized nations. They are making the decisions on investment and development. They are responsible for material production, essential economic services, and a large part of social services. The state simply collects taxes and then distributes and spends them. In many of these countries, the entire could go on vacation and nobody would even notice.

The developed capitalist system, which later gave rise to modern imperialism, has now imposed a neoliberal and globalized order that is simply unsustainable. It has created a world of speculation, in which fictitious wealth and stocks have been created that have nothing to do with actual production. It has created enormous personal fortunes, some of which exceed the gross domestic product of dozens of poor countries. This is not to mention the plunder and squander of the world's natural resources or the miserable lives of billions of people. There is nothing this system can offer humanity. It can only lead to its own self-destruction and perhaps along with it, the destruction of the natural conditions that sustain human life on this planet.

The end of history, predicted by a few euphoric dreamers, is not here, yet. Perhaps history is just beginning.

Forty-one years after the revolution, and despite all of the difficulties it has had to confront, the regime that you established has endured. What could be the reason for this longevity?

Fidel Castro — Tireless struggle and work alongside the people and for the people. The fact that we have convictions and have acted accordingly; that we believe in humankind and in being our country's slaves and not its masters. We believe in building upon solid principles; in seeking out and producing solutions, even in apparently impossible conditions, and in preserving the honesty of those with the highest political and administrative responsibilities — that is, in transforming politics into a priesthood. This could be a partial answer to your question, setting aside many other elements particularly related to our country and this historical era.

Of course, everybody thought that Cuba would not survive the collapse of the socialist camp and the Soviet Union. One could certainly wonder how it was possible to withstand a double blockade and the economic and political warfare unleashed against our country by the mightiest power ever, without the IMF [International Monetary Fund] or the World Bank, without credits. We managed, however, to achieve this feat. At a summit meeting recently held in Havana, I said to our guests somewhat ironically that it was actually possible because we had the privilege of not being IMF members.

There were times when Cuba was swimming in a sea of circulating money. Our national currency experienced an extraordinary devaluation, and the budget deficit reached 35 percent of our gross domestic product. I could see intelligent visitors almost faint from shock. Our peso, the national currency, dropped in 1994 to a value of 150 to the dollar. In spite of this, we did not close down a single health care center, a single school or daycare center, a single university or a single sports facility. Nobody was fired and left on their own without employment or social security, even when fuel and raw materials were most scarce. There were no traces of the customary and hideous shock policies so highly recommended by the Western financial institutions.

Every measure adopted to confront the terrible blow was discussed not only in the National Assembly, but also in hundreds of thousands of assemblies held in factories, centers of production and services, trade unions, universities, secondary schools and farmers', women's and neighbors' organizations as well as in other social groups. The little that was available, we distributed as equitably as possible. Pessimism was overcome both inside and outside the country.

During those critical years, the number of doctors doubled, and the quality of education improved. Between 1994 and 1998, the value of the Cuban peso increased sevenfold, from 150 to 20 to the dollar, and has since remained consistently stable. Not a single dollar fled the country. We acquired enough experience and efficiency to face such an immense challenge. Although we still have not reached the production and consumption levels we had before the demise of socialism in Europe, we have gradually recovered at a steady and visible pace. Our education, health and social security rates, as well as many other social features, which were the pride of our country, have been preserved, and some have even been improved.

The great hero in this feat has been the people, who have contributed tremendous sacrifices and immense trust. Our survival has been the result of justice and of the ideas planted over 40 years of revolution. This genuine miracle would have been impossible without unity and without socialism.

In view of the vast movement towards globalization taking place worldwide, would it not perhaps be advisable to open up more of the Cuban economy to the rest of the world?
Fidel Castro — We have opened up the economy to the extent that it has been possible and necessary. We have not gone for the same insanities and follies as in other places, where the recommendations of European and U.S. experts have been followed as if they were

biblical prophecies. We have not been driven by the insanity of privatization, and much less by that of confiscating state property to take it over ourselves or hand it out in gifts to relatives or friends. This happened, as we all know, both in former socialist countries and in others that were never socialist, under the pious, tolerant, and complicit cover of neoliberal philosophy that has become a universal pandemic. The West is well aware of where the money is deposited and what has happened to embezzled or stolen funds, but nobody says a word about it.

We have not attempted the folly of adapting Cuba to today's chaotic world, or its philosophy. We have adapted those realities to our own, while at the same time fighting alongside many other countries of the so-called Third World for our right to development and survival. This is perhaps the way for our former colonies to help the minority of very wealthy countries, most of them former colonial powers, to save themselves as well.

Nobody questions Cuba's social and cultural achievements. However, returning to my previous question, would these achievements not be better served by an increase in exchange with the outside world?
Fidel Castro — It's true that, as you say, we have achieved major social advances. This could hardly be denied. There is schooling for all of our children, and no illiteracy. The development of our universities is considerable. We have numerous research centers carrying out important, high-quality work. Every child is given 13 vaccines, almost all of them produced in our own country, as is the case with most of the medicines we use. At the same time, thousands of our doctors are providing their services, free of charge, in remote and impoverished areas of Latin America, the Caribbean and Africa, in comprehensive health care programs. This is possible because we have plenty of human capital.

We have invited the most developed countries to cooperate by sending medications. We are also granting thousands of scholarships for young Third World people to study medicine and other specialized courses in our universities. In every African country participating in the health care programs, we are helping to establish schools that can eventually train the hundreds of thousands of doctors they need.

It's difficult to imagine what a small Third World country with

extremely limited resources can achieve when a true spirit of solidarity prevails. As to your question, there is no doubt that the efforts
undertaken by our country could be boosted by an increase in
exchanges with the outside world, to the benefit both of Cuba and
other nations.

*The demise of the Soviet Union suddenly deprived Cuba of precious aid. In
your opinion, what was the US purpose in maintaining the embargo despite
the end of the East-West confrontation? Did they hope to influence your
form of government?*

Fidel Castro — They were not trying to influence the revolution but
to destroy it. Just as in Hannibal's times when the Senate in ancient
Rome proclaimed the destruction of Carthage, the obsessively
pursued motto of U.S. administrations has been: Cuba must be
destroyed.

The demise of the Soviet Union and the collapse of the European
socialist bloc did not take us completely by surprise. We had long
before warned our people of this possibility. The stupid mistakes
and shameful concessions they constantly made to their longstanding
enemy clearly pointed to what was coming.

In economic terms, Cuba sustained terrible damage. The price
we had been paid for our sugar was not that prevailing in the unfair
world market. We had obtained a preferential price, in the same
way the United States grants preferences to Europe for their imports
of this commodity. Supplies of fuel, food, raw material and parts for
machinery and factories were abruptly and almost completely cut
off. The daily intake of calories dropped from 3,000 to 1,900, and
that of protein from 80 to 50 grams. Some people could not put up
with the difficulties, but the immense majority confronted the
hardships with remarkable courage, honor and determination.

As I said earlier, we managed to maintain important achievements, and some were even improved. In this 10 year period, infant
mortality was reduced and 30,000 new medical doctors went to work
in our communities. In the field of sports, our athletes continued to
occupy a place among the world's best, with the highest number of
gold medals per capita in the Olympics, despite tremendous pressure
from the United States and other wealthy countries who were
attempting to entice Cuban scientists, professionals and athletes to
leave Cuba.

But the continuation of the embargo is not another test that the Cuban people can easily overcome.

Fidel Castro — The blockade, of course, is a painful burden for each and every Cuban. The Third World nations, and most other UN member countries, have repeatedly demanded the lifting of the blockade. But the U.S. Congress, with the cooperation of many members of the Republican majority, headed up in this case by Mr. Helms and Mr. Burton, and even with the support of several Democratic Party members, such as Mr. Torricelli, has opposed the lifting of the blockade, which is by far the longest lasting in history.

The United States is not the only country imposing all sorts of conditions on your country. The European Union has also tried to introduce a "democracy clause" in European-Cuban trade relations. What do you think of this action?

Fidel Castro — It is significant that the European Union shows much less "concern" about other countries, doubtlessly because they are of a greater economic interest than we ever could be. In any case, all conditions become unacceptable when the inalienable principles of our homeland are involved. The political organization adopted by a sovereign nation cannot be subjected to conditions. Cuba will neither negotiate nor sell out its revolution, which has cost the lives of many of its sons and daughters.

Alternatively, it depends on what is meant by a "democracy clause." How many so-called "democratic" states are up to their necks in debt? How many of them allow up to 30 percent of the population to live in conditions of extreme poverty? Why should countries with tens of thousands of children wandering the streets and countless numbers of illiterate people, be treated better than we are? We do not see why this should be so. Cuba will never accept political conditions from the European Union, and much less from the United States. This should be definitely understood.

We do not argue about whether the countries in Europe are monarchies or republics, or whether power is held by conservatives or social democrats, advocates or adversaries of an idyllic third option; swings to the left, to the center or to the right; supporters or detractors of the so-called "welfare state" used as a palliative for the incurable disease of unemployment. We do not feel the urge to express our views on the actions of the skinheads and the upsurge of neo-Nazi tendencies. Although we have our own ideas about these and many other issues, we do not introduce revolutionary clauses in our relations with Europe. We rather hope the Europeans will work things out by themselves.

Since the days of McCarthyism, Washington has tended to consider that the only regimes that are harmful and must be eliminated are communist regimes. But the White House has tolerated, without blinking, the likes of Somoza [Nicaragua], Trujillo [the Dominican Republic], Duvalier [Haiti] and others. What are your thoughts on this "double-standard" approach?
Fidel Castro — It would be better not to delve into the hypocrisy and indecency of that policy. It would take many hours and lengthy historical references.

The market will dry up some day for the industry of lies, it is drying up already. If you really delve into the truth, you will realize that the political conception of imperialism, as well as the neoliberal economic order and globalization process imposed on the world, is orphaned and defenseless when it comes to ideas and ethics. It is in this field that the main struggle of our times will be decided. And the final result of this battle, with no possible alternative, will be on the side of truth, and thus on the side of humanity.

How far can the privatization process go in Cuba? As for the "dollarization" of the economy, isn't this an insult both to socialism and the country's monetary sovereignty?
Fidel Castro — I have already said that privatization should be carried out with a great deal of common sense and wisdom, avoiding irrational actions. You need to make a clear distinction between different kinds of work. Some tasks are highly individual and often manual and craft-like; their large-scale production and technology are not fundamental. However, there are investments that require capital, technology and markets, in which associations with foreign companies can be highly advisable. The potential oil deposits in the 110,000 square kilometers of the Gulf of Mexico belonging to Cuba could not be explored or exploited by our country without technology and capital from abroad.

Within the country, however, when it comes to obtaining the highest quality and yield in special crops like tobacco — the work of dedicated and almost fanatical lovers of this type of farming, which should be manual and carried out on small plots of land — no machine or big company could replace the individual's work. Those people with these special qualities are given the land they need, free of charge, in order to farm it on their own. It would be absurd to do the same with huge sugarcane plantations that are highly mechanized.

In the Cuban farming sector, there are different forms of ownership: individual property, cooperatives and various forms of collective production. At the same time, in a wide range of economic sectors, there are production and marketing associations with foreign companies that work perfectly well.

When it comes to privatization, one should not be simplistic. The general principle in Cuba is: if something is possible and advisable to preserve as the property of the people or a collective of workers, it will not be privatized.

Our ideology and our preference is socialist, which bears no relation whatsoever to the selfishness, privileges and inequalities of capitalist society. In Cuba, nothing will pass into the hands of a high ranking official, and nothing will be given away to accomplices and friends. Nothing that can be efficiently exploited for the benefit of our society will pass into the hands of either Cuban or foreign individuals. At the same time, I can assure you that the safest investments in the world are those authorized in Cuba, which are protected by law and by the country's honor.

I should say two things in reference to the "dollarization" of the economy. Firstly, the world economy is currently dollarized. After Bretton Woods [1944 Conference to establish the IMF and the International Bank for Reconstruction and Development], the United States acquired the privilege of issuing the reserve currency of the world economy. Secondly, there is a national currency in Cuba that is not ruled in any way by the IMF. As I noted earlier, that currency has experienced a sevenfold increase in value, in record time. There has been no flight of capital.

At the same time, a convertible peso has been established, on a par with the dollar, whose free circulation was simply an unavoidable need, not the result of an economic concession. I believe that in the future it will never again be necessary to ban the possession of dollars or other foreign currencies, but its free circulation for the payment of many goods and services will only last as long as the interests of the revolution make it advisable. We are not concerned about the famous phrase "the dollarization of the economy." We know very well what we are doing.

Fidel, you publicly said to me in Havana in 1997: "Federico, today there is no need for revolutions. As of now, the struggle will be for better sharing. Our objective is no longer the class struggle but the rapprochement of the classes within the framework of just and peaceful coexistence." Three years later, do you still think the same way?

Fidel Castro — I am not sure that I ever made those exact comments. It might have been a misunderstanding associated to voice inflexion or a misinterpretation, because some of those points are quite distant from my ideas.

I recently attended an international economists' meeting in Havana. Among participants there were representatives of financially distressed countries where debt servicing accounts for over 40 percent of budget spending. Previous and acting governments acquired such debts "very democratically." There is clearly a great sense of helplessness in the face of challenges posed by this inevitable globalization process, marked so far by the fatal signs of neo-liberalism. At the meeting, representatives of the Inter-American Development Bank and the World Bank defended their points of view with complete freedom, but for many of those present, the conclusions were very clear regarding the unsustainable nature of the prevailing economic order.

It is not possible to continue along the path that widens the gap between poor and rich countries and produces increasingly serious social inequalities within them all. At the moment, Latin American and Caribbean integration is fundamental. It is only by joining together that we can negotiate our role in this hemisphere. The same applies to the Third World countries vis-à-vis the powerful and insatiable club of the wealthy. I have often noted that such integration and the joining of forces cannot wait for profound social changes or social revolutions to take place within these individual countries.

I have also said that because the current world economic order is unsustainable, it faces the very real danger of a catastrophic collapse, infinitely worse than the disaster and prolonged crisis set off in 1929 by the crash of the U.S. stock markets, where stocks had been inflated beyond sustainable levels. Not even the enthusiastic and highly experienced Allan Greenspan, chairman of the U.S. Federal Reserve — whose sleepless eyes do not stray for a minute from statistics that emanate from the uncontrollable, unpredictable roulette wheel of the speculative system, in which 50 percent of U.S. families have placed their bets and invested their savings — would dare to claim that this danger does not exist. The remedy to prevent it has not been invented, and it cannot be invented within such a system.

I tirelessly insist on the need for people to open their eyes to these realities. A collapse could occur before the people are prepared for it. Changes will not spring forth from any one person's head, but all of the heads must be prepared for inevitable changes, which will take on a wide variety of forms and follow a wide variety of paths. From my point of view, these changes will fundamentally result from the action of the masses, which nothing will succeed in holding back.

Nevertheless, nothing will be easy. The blindness, superficiality and irresponsibility of the so-called political class will make the road more difficult, but not impregnable.

Is there any hope for the poor to achieve a better life in the next 20 years?
Fidel Castro — Humanity is beginning to gain awareness. Look at what happened in Seattle and in Davos.

People frequently talk about the horrors of the holocaust and the genocides that have taken place throughout the century, but they seem to forget that every year, as a result of the economic order we have been discussing here, tens of millions of people starve to death or die of preventable diseases. They can wield statistics of apparently positive growth, but in the end things in the Third World countries remain the same or even worsen. Growth often rests on the accumulation of consumer goods that contribute nothing to true development or to a better distribution of wealth. The truth is that after several decades of neoliberalism, the rich are becoming increasingly rich while the poor are both more numerous and increasingly poor.

At the recent summit of the Group of 77 held in April [2000] in Havana, you put forward a series of ideas to reform the international order. Could you repeat those proposals?
Fidel Castro — At the summit, I advocated for the cancelation of the least developed countries' external debt and for a considerable debt

relief for many others. I also spoke out for the removal of the IMF. It is time that the Third World countries demand to be freed from a mechanism that has not ensured the stability of the world economy. In general, I censured the fatal impact of hypocritical neoliberal policies on every underdeveloped country, particularly the Latin American and Caribbean countries. I said that another Nuremberg trial was needed, to pass sentence on the genocide committed by the current world economic order.

That is a bit of an overstatement!
Fidel Castro — Perhaps not. It might be a bit of an understatement. For the sake of precision, I shall quote a few paragraphs from my closing speech at the South Summit:

"People used to talk about apartheid in South Africa. Today we could talk about apartheid throughout the world, where over four billion people are deprived of the most basic rights of all human beings: the right to life, health, education, clean drinking water, food, housing, employment, hope for their future and the future of their children. At the present pace, we will soon be deprived even of the air we breathe, increasingly poisoned as it is by wasteful consumer societies that pollute the elements that are essential for life and destroy human habitat...

"The wealthy world tries to forget that the sources of under-development and poverty are slavery, colonialism and the brutal exploitation to which our countries were subjected for centuries. They look upon us as inferior nations. They attribute the poverty we suffer to the inability of Africans, Asians, Caribbeans and Latin Americans, in other words, of black-skinned, yellow-skinned, indigenous and mixed-race peoples, to achieve any degree of development, or even to govern ourselves...

"I am firmly convinced that the current economic order imposed by the wealthy countries is not only cruel, unfair, inhuman, and contrary to the inevitable course of history but is also inherently racist. It reflects racist conceptions like those that once inspired the Nazi holocaust and concentration camps in Europe, mirrored today in the Third World's so-called refugee camps, which actually serve to concentrate the effects of poverty, hunger and violence. These are the same racist conceptions that inspired the hateful system of apartheid in Africa...

"We are fighting for the most sacred rights of the poor countries; but we are also fighting for the salvation of a First World incapable of preserving the existence of the human species. Overwhelmed by contradictions and self-serving interests, it is incapable of governing itself, and much less of governing the world, whose leadership must be democratically shared. We are fighting — it could almost be demonstrated mathematically — to preserve life on our planet."

In summary, Federico: it is urgent that we fight for our survival, the survival of all countries, both rich and poor, because we are all in the same boat. In this regard, I made a very concrete proposal at the summit concerning a delicate and complex issue: I asked the Third World oil-exporting countries to grant preferential prices to the least developed countries, similar to what was done in the San José Pact, signed 20 years ago by Venezuela and Mexico, which allows Central American and Caribbean countries to buy oil on more lenient terms.

Is your opinion about the United Nations as severe?
Fidel Castro — Not at all, although I consider its structure an anachronism. After 55 years of existence, it is essential to reestablish the organization. The United Nations should be worthy of its name: the members should be truly united by genuinely humane and far-reaching objectives. All of the member countries, big and small, developed and underdeveloped, should have the real possibility of making their voices heard. The United Nations should constitute a great meeting place, where all views can be expressed and discussed. It should operate on truly democratic bases. It is important for groups like the G-77 and the Nonaligned Nations Movement to act within the UN system.

The UN structure should be transformed, so that the organization can play a major role in today's world. Social development, for example, is presently one of the most dramatically urgent needs in the Third World. The mission of the World Bank is not to contribute funds to resolve financial crises but rather to promote social development. The absence of such development is the greatest tragedy of our times.

Looking at a world map, what changes would you like to make?
Fidel Castro — I would be thinking of a world worthy of the human

species, without hyper-wealthy and wasteful nations on the one hand and countless countries mired in extreme poverty on the other; a world in which all identities and cultures were preserved; a world with justice and solidarity; a world without plundering, oppression or wars, where science and technology were at the service of human-kind; a world where nature was protected and the great throng of people living on the planet today could survive, grow and enjoy the spiritual and material wealth that talent and labor could create. No need to ask — I dream of a world that the capitalist philosophy will never make possible.

What do you think of the evolution of Latin America as a whole?
Fidel Castro — I think that it is behind almost 200 years in its social development and political integration. Some Latin American countries have a great many more economic resources than Cuba, which has been blockaded for over 40 years now. But if you take a good look at them, it turns out that in many of these countries a third of the population cannot read or write, that millions of Latin Americans lack even a roof to shelter them, that these countries are so highly indebted, their development is practically impossible.

The Latin American debt is so large that many nations in the region, no matter what their gross domestic product may be, do not guarantee a decent quality of life to most of their people. Their economies, which sometimes appear to be doing well according to macroeconomic figures, have fallen prey to major financial and technological powers. All of these economies are subject to flights of capital to wealthy countries, in amounts that nobody fully knows or can calculate. Their weak currencies are defenseless against the attacks of speculators. The hard currency reserves with which they attempt to defend their economies are lost in a matter of days when faced with any danger of devaluation. Incomes earned through a privatization that gives away national heritage are lost without providing the slightest benefit. The threat of financial crisis or devaluation turns all forms of capital into "flight-overnight" capital, including both short-term loans and the funds of nationals terrified by the imminent risk of watching their savings dwindle.

Latin America, like the rest of the Third World, is a victim of the imposed international economic order, which I have already described as unsustainable. The handy formula of endlessly raising interest rates creates chaos for the economic life of these countries. The countries of Latin America, divided and Balkanized, are seduced by the siren song of a hemispheric free trade agreement that emanates deceptive illusions of progress and development. They are in danger of forever losing their independence and of being annexed by the United States.

I would now like to address a rather sensitive issue: that of freedom of expression and freedom of thought. The Cuban regime is regularly attacked for its repressive policy with regard to...

Fidel Castro — I can guess what you were going to say. First, I wonder if it is fair to discuss freedom of expression and thought in a region where the immense majority of the people are either totally or functionally illiterate. It sounds like a cruel joke, but it is much worse.

Many people in the world not only lack freedom of thought but also the capacity to think, because it has been destroyed. Billions of human beings, including a large percentage of those living in developed societies, are told what brand of soda they should drink, what cigarettes they should smoke, what clothes and shoes they should wear, what they should eat and what brand of food they should buy. Their political ideas are supplied in the same way.

Every year, a trillion dollars is spent on advertising. This rain pours on the masses that are deprived of the necessary elements of judgment to formulate opinions. This has never happened before in the history of humanity. Primitive humans enjoyed greater freedom of thought. José Martí said, "To be educated in order to be free." We would have to add a dictum: freedom is impossible without culture. Education and culture are what the revolution has offered in abundance to our people, much more so than in a large number of the developed countries.

Living in a consumer society does not necessarily make people educated. It is amazing, sometimes, how superficial and simplistic their knowledge can be. Cuba has raised the average educational level of its people to ninth grade, just as a beginning. In 10 years, average cultural levels will be those of university graduates. All of the necessary conditions have been created. No one can prevent our people from becoming the most cultivated, or from having a profound political culture that is neither dogmatic nor sectarian, something that is severely lacking in many of the world's wealthiest nations. We will place at the service of this lofty goal the great technologies created by humankind, while avoiding commercial advertising.

It would perhaps be better to wait a while before talking about true freedom of expression and thought, because that can never be reconciled with a brutal economic and social capitalist system that fails to respect culture, solidarity and ethics.

For several years now, we have seen an embryo of opposition being born in Cuba; that is, dissident groups are beginning to organize. This being the case, is it not perhaps time for the Cuban regime to open up to political pluralism?

Fidel Castro — Opposition emerged when, in the midst of the Cold War and only 90 miles from the United States, our profound social revolution was made. The United States has organized and directed that opposition for over 40 years.

The revolution did away with centuries of privilege and affected the interests of the wealthiest and most influential sectors of Cuban society; it also affected the large agricultural, mining, industrial, commercial and service companies that the United States had established in Cuba. Our country has been the target of a dirty war, mercenary invasions and threats of direct military attacks. We were also on the brink of a nuclear war.

The leader of that extensive counterrevolutionary activity and the economic, political and ideological war that followed was and continues to be the government of the United States of America. The rest is pure fiction, artificially created and always well financed by that superpower, its allies and its lackeys.

The counterrevolution is wrapped up in lies and slander, which constitute the backbone of a system devoid of ideas and ethics. It is confronting a revolution that has already faced, endured and passed the hardest tests, and a united, combative and politically stronger people.

There will be no such opening. We do not see why we should cooperate with the U.S. strategy.

The majority of your ministers had not been born when the armed revolution triumphed.

Fidel Castro — It shows that they are young and that the revolution will be around for a while.

What are the dreams of the Cuban people today?
Fidel Castro — I think there are 11 million dreams.

In what way are they different from the dreams of the previous generation?
Fidel Castro — Before, they each dreamed of their own happiness. Today, they all dream of happiness for everyone.

Would you not like to link the people more closely to the political decision-making process?
Fidel Castro — Do you really think that Cuba and the revolution would exist without a maximum degree of people's participation?

Since the triumph of the revolution, a tenth of the Cuban population has left the island. How do you explain this exodus?
Fidel Castro — You mentioned figures. I am trying to recall the various migrations from Cuba and it seems to me that the figures are lower, except if they include those who were born abroad. In any case, that is not so important.

Before the revolution, the number of U.S. visas granted to Cubans was insignificant. When the revolution triumphed, the doors were opened wide. Of the 6,000 doctors we had, they took away half, along with a number of university professors and teachers. It was a major extraction of human resources. We firmly withstood the blow. No one was prevented from emigrating. It was not us, but them: they closed the doors on more than one occasion and established quotas for legal emigration. Their worst crime has been to encourage illegal emigration with the Cuban Adjustment Act, by virtue of which any person, regardless of his or her legal background or conduct, who illegally leaves Cuba and by any means arrives in U.S. territory, is given the right to residency in that country. They have received many criminals in this way — although not all those who leave are criminals — and many people have lost their lives. It was this law, the only one of its kind in the world, created solely for Cubans, that led to the case of the kidnapped boy Elián González, who was not even six years old at the time of the misadventure in which 11 Cubans lost their lives, his mother included.

If the same privileges had been extended to Mexico and the rest of Latin America and the Caribbean throughout almost 35 years, more than half of the people in the United States would be Latin American and Caribbean. Mexico and the United States would not be separated today by a wall higher than that in Berlin. More would-be-emigrants perish every year attempting to cross the Mexico-U.S. border than those who died in all the years that the Berlin wall existed. Let these privileges be offered in Europe to the people living North and South of the Sahara, and let's see how many emigrate.

It should be said that we have never prohibited emigration from Cuba to the United States, and that 90 percent of those who have emigrated have done so for economic reasons.

The case of little Elián has inflamed the passions of the Cuban exile community in Miami. What is your opinion of Cuban dissidents, both within the island and in Florida?
Fidel Castro — I do not see the difference between what you call external and internal dissidents. They are exactly the same thing. They both have the same origin and the same leadership. Both are instruments of U.S. policy against Cuba, both are pro-imperialist, antisocialist and in favor of annexation. Those who were promoted as leaders of the so-called Cuban American National Foundation — an abomination that emerged from the Santa Fe Document, the Republican Party's 1980 political platform on Cuba — were almost without exception former CIA members or the children of well-known war criminals who had escaped to the United States when the revolution triumphed.

The list of crimes and misdeeds they committed against Cuba is endless, first as individuals recruited at the time of the [1961] Bay of Pigs mercenary invasion, and later as members of the aforementioned Cuban American mafia. One of the goals of Reagan and his team was to have a political surrogate that, supposedly in the name of Cuban representatives, would put forward pieces of legislation or measures related to the blockade and the economic warfare against our homeland. They were granted contracts and economic concessions. They trafficked in everything, including drugs, and amassed huge fortunes. One of their most important missions was the inception of a lobby to promote and sponsor allies and the most reactionary people from the extreme right from either of the two parties in Congress. Their arsenal of actions against Cuba included supporting apparently independent terrorist groups to carry out various acts of sabotage against the economy, political crimes and the introduction of pests and biological warfare. They organized their own military apparatus and concocted countless plots to assassinate me whenever I traveled abroad — with the full knowledge and tolerance of the U.S. authorities. They had abundant resources available to them, and handed out campaign funds to dozens of lawmakers from both parties, both over and under the table. They managed to put up legislators from their own group and helped to elect others. Official support was unqualified.

It is outrageous to think about everything they have done against our homeland. Their most recent crime was the kidnapping of a child from his legitimate family. As the owners of Florida, they felt they had the right to defy the laws and orders of the federal government itself. They trampled and burned U.S. flags. The enormously stupid misdeed committed in the case of this Cuban boy has been their political Waterloo. It will be very difficult for them to pick up the scattered pieces of considerable power and political influence they had achieved, to put together something new that will be able to serve them.

The other arm of the U.S. counterrevolutionary strategy, the small groupings promoted over the years to create an internal front against the revolution, is just as morally and politically destroyed. They spur on these groups with funds that arrive by a wide range of means, and support them with all the media in their reach. These groups promote their counterrevolutionary and slanderous campaigns through the subversive radio stations broadcasting out of the United States and the [Cuban American National] Foundation-controlled press. They work in close alliance with the Cuban American mafia and are directly coordinated by the staff of the U.S. Interests Section in Havana, by Czech and Polish diplomats and by other officials from the embassies of several countries allied with or subordinated to the United States.

Their essential mission is to obstruct Cuba's diplomatic and economic relations, and to use their provocation to supply publicity material for propaganda and slander campaigns aimed at isolating Cuba. In these glorious and heroic years of double blockade and "special period," when the survival of our homeland is at stake, the feats achieved by our people will submerge them into the swamp of their own infamy, and into what is the most certain and worthy fate for their shameful role: oblivion.

How did you react to the condemnation of Cuba in the UN Human Rights Commission on April 18, 2000: the result of an initiative of the Czech Republic and Poland? You were reproached for violently repressing political dissidents and religious groups...

Fidel Castro — Regarding the vote in Geneva, it was obviously the case of a new and hypocritical act of U.S. hostility and aggression against Cuba. Actively complicit governments from a few former socialist countries, willing to play the U.S. dirty game, with the support of their European accomplices, voted as a bloc in Geneva alongside their powerful ally and boss of NATO.

We did not hesitate to expose this infamous maneuver. Our people condemned it unanimously and we formulated resounding denunciations against those involved in the plot, many of whom have not been able to respond. Reactions will be increasingly tough, and the battle against Cuba increasingly difficult.

Pope John Paul II visited Havana in January of 1998. Did he convince you?

Fidel Castro — I really do not recall the Pope trying to convince me of anything. We received him with the hospitality and respect deserved by such an outstanding personality, one with special talent and charisma. We both spoke in public upon his arrival and departure, and we both put forward our ideas with respect and dignity.

We handed the country over to him. We provided him with the most historic public squares, which were chosen by the organizers of the visit. Our television networks were available to him. We provided the transportation requested for mobilizations, using all of the means available in our blockaded country. We invited the mass organizations, members of our party and the Union of Young Communists to attend the masses, under strict instructions to listen respectfully to everything the Pope had to say, with no placards, slogans, or revolutionary shouts. To report the visit throughout the world, 110 foreign television networks and 5,000 journalists received permission to document his visit. There was not a single soldier on the streets, or a single armed police officer. Nothing like this has ever happened anywhere else in the world.

At the end, the organizers stated that it was the best organized visit the Pope had ever made. Not a single traffic accident occurred. I think that he took away a good impression of our country; at the same time, he made a good impression on Cuba. I had the opportunity to admire his working capacity and his dedication to strictly complying with the grueling itinerary worked out by his staff. The only ones faced with a fiasco were those individuals abroad — and there were quite a few of them — who thought that with the mere presence of the Pope, the revolution would fall like the walls of Jericho. In the end, both the revolution and the Pope emerged very much aware of their own strengths.

No one is immortal, neither heads of state nor common men and women. Do you not think that it would be wise to prepare a successor, even if it is only to spare the Cuban people the trauma of a chaotic transition?
Fidel Castro — I am very much aware that humans are mortal but I have never worried about it, although it has been a key factor in my life. When my rebellious nature led me to the dangerous calling of a revolutionary fighter, something that no one forced me into, I also knew that there was very little chance I could survive for long. I was not a head of state but a very common individual. I did not inherit a position, and I am not a king. Therefore, I do not need to prepare a successor. In any case, it would never be to prevent the trauma of a chaotic transition. There will be no trauma, or the need for any kind of transition.

The transition from one social system to another has been taking place for over 40 years. This is not about replacing one human with another.

When a genuine revolution has been consolidated and when ideas and consciousness have begun to bear fruit, no human is indispensable, no matter how important his or her personal contribution may have been. There is no cult of personality in Cuba. You will never see official photographs, or streets or parks or schools named after living leaders. The responsibilities are very well shared and the work is distributed among many. A large number of young and already experienced people, together with a small group of older revolutionaries, with whom they closely identify, will be the ones who keep the country going. It cannot be overlooked that there is a party here with great prestige and moral authority. So what is there to worry about?

What you are saying is perfectly true. However, precisely by not putting into place right now the individuals and structures, that is, the relief force that can take over when the time comes, do you not think that you are increasing the risk that these social achievements will be questioned?
Fidel Castro — The relief force as you have called it is not only already prepared but it has also been in place and working for quite some time.

It is your privilege to be a living myth. Will you continue to be a myth after you pass away?
Fidel Castro — I am not a myth. Successive U.S. administrations have turned me into what you call a myth and if I have been a living myth, it is also thanks to the failure of their countless attempts to cut my life short. But, of course, I will continue to be one after I am dead. Would it really be possible to dismiss the merit of having struggled for so many years against such a powerful empire?

Fidel Castro, always the conspirator. Does this image belong to an obsolete past?
Fidel Castro — On the contrary, it has become such a significant habit of mine that I do not even talk to myself about the most important secret strategies in our revolutionary struggle. I prefer to talk about them on television.

Why do you live by night? When do you prepare your speeches?
Fidel Castro — I live and almost always work at all hours, day and night. Can you really afford to waste time once you are over 70? As for my speeches, I have come to the conclusion, a bit late perhaps, that speeches ought to be short.

2

"The dream of having truly fair and sensible rules to guide human destiny seems impossible to many. However, we are convinced that struggling for the impossible should be the motto of this institution that brings us together today!"

Address to the Millennium Summit of the United Nations, New York
September 6, 2000

Chaos rules in our world, both within countries' borders and beyond. Blind laws are offered up as divine norms that would bring the peace, order, well-being and security our planet so badly needs. That is what they would have us believe.

Three dozen developed and wealthy nations that monopolize economic, political and technological power have joined us in this gathering to offer the same recipes that have only served to make us poorer, more exploited and more dependent. There is not even discussion about radical reform of this old institution — born over a half century ago when there were few independent nations — to turn it into a body truly representative of the interests of all the peoples on Earth; an institution where no one would have the disturbing and undemocratic right of veto and where a transparent process could be undertaken to expand membership and representation in the Security Council. It is an executive body subordinated to the General Assembly, which should be the one making the decisions on such crucial issues as intervention and the use of force.

It should be clearly stated that the principle of sovereignty cannot be sacrificed to the might and strength of a superpower that under an abusive and unfair order tries to decide everything by itself. That sacrifice, Cuba will never accept.

The poverty and underdevelopment prevailing in most nations as well as inequality in the distribution of wealth and knowledge in the world are basically at the source of the present conflicts. It cannot be forgotten that current underdevelopment and poverty have resulted from conquest, colonization, slavery and plunder by the colonial powers in most countries of the planet and from the emergence of imperialism and the brutal wars motivated by new divisions of the world. Today, it is their moral obligation to compensate our nations for the damage caused throughout centuries.

Humanity should be aware of what we have been so far and what we cannot continue to be. Currently, our species has enough accumulated knowledge, ethical values and scientific resources to move toward a new historical era of true justice and humanism.

There is nothing in the existing economic and political order that can serve the interests of humankind. It is unsustainable and it must be changed. Suffice it to say that the world's population is already six billion people, 80 percent of whom live in poverty. Age old diseases of the Third World nations such as malaria, tuberculosis and others equally lethal have not yet been eradicated, while new epidemics like AIDS threaten to exterminate the population of entire nations. On the other hand, wealthy countries continue to invest enormous amounts of money in the military and in luxury items. A voracious plague of speculators exchange currencies, stocks and other real or fictitious values for trillions of dollars every day.

Nature is being devastated. The climate is changing under our own eyes and drinking water is increasingly scarce or contaminated. The sources of our seafood are being depleted and crucial nonrenewable resources are wasted in luxury and triviality.

Anyone should be able to understand that the basic role of the

United Nations in the pressing new century is to save the world not only from war but also from underdevelopment, hunger, disease, poverty and the destruction of natural resources indispensable to human life. It should do so promptly before it is too late!

The dream of having truly fair and sensible rules to guide human destiny seems impossible to many. However, we are convinced that struggling for the impossible should be the motto of this institution that brings us together today!

3

"More than a few African representatives expressed a hard reality: that even if [AIDS] medications were donated, their countries lack the infrastructure to distribute and administer them."

The Tragedy of AIDS in the Third World, UN Millennium Summit, New York
September 7, 2000

I have meditated a great deal about the seriousness of this subject. I think it has been discussed for more than 40 years, and actually, we haven't progressed but rather gone backwards.

There is proof of what I say: At the present time, in more than 100 countries, per capita income is lower than it was 15 years ago.

Everybody here has expounded the ideas they most wished to transmit within the brief time available, and I would like to say that I am profoundly affected by issues related to the disastrous state of health currently affecting the world, particularly in the Third World countries. I don't really like using a lot of figures, but nevertheless, I will.

Life expectancy in sub-Saharan Africa is barely 48 years. This is

30 years less than in the developed countries. In terms of the maternal death rate, 99.5 percent of all such deaths occur in the Third World.

The risk of maternal death in Europe is one per 1,400 births; in Africa it is one per 16. The general mortality rate is similar.

More than 11 million children under five die every year in the Third World as a result, in the overwhelming majority of cases, of preventable diseases: more than 30,000 every day, 21 every minute. While we are talking here, 100 are dying.

Two out of every five children in Third World countries suffer from retarded growth, and one out of every three is underweight in relation to age.

Two million female children are forced into prostitution. In the underdeveloped countries, approximately 250 million children under the age of 15 are obliged to work in order to survive.

Many people have also talked here on the issue of AIDS. I had the impression some months ago, at the Durban meeting, that the tragedy of AIDS in Africa had been discovered by the West. At that conference, as was widely reported by the news agencies, there was talk of how to reduce the cost of medical care for persons infected with AIDS and how to keep them alive. We know that to buy the medicines and treatment one infected person needs, it costs $10,000. Yet it is also known that to produce the medications costs close to $1,000 per person with AIDS. With a perfect formula and a perfect cocktail of drugs, even that cost could be greatly reduced.

It was affirmed by representatives from the Western nations, European countries generally, that cost-saving formulas had to be sought. I have heard representatives from industrialized countries like France, Sweden, Germany and others also express their disposition to help these Third World countries. But more than a few African representatives expressed a hard reality: that even if medications were donated, their countries lack the infrastructure to distribute and administer them.

This is a question of life or death. I have been asking myself: what can we do? I remind you that Cuba is a small country, and poor. And something else: besieged and blockaded, but I don't want to talk to you about that. Thanks to intensive educational programs that have been developed over many years, Cuba now has significant human capital, and human capital is decisive. I would say it is even more important than financial capital. Our country has sufficient medical personnel to cooperate — if the United Nations agrees — with the World Health Organization and the peoples of sub-Saharan Africa, who are suffering from this destructive scourge to the greatest degree, in order to organize the infrastructure needed to administer those medications in Africa on an emergency basis. I am not exaggerating. This could signify 1,000 doctors, and 2,000 or 3,000 health workers, including paramedics who would be needed to collectively undertake that program.

We don't have to wait for millions of children to die. A good proportion of the 25 million people infected could survive, averting the growing number of orphans. Already close to 12 million, the figure in another few years will increase to 40 million — a Dantean tragedy!

No country, whatever its resources, can develop with 25 to 30 percent of its population infected with AIDS, and millions and millions of orphans. In my view, AIDS signifies the extermination of entire African nations, and possibly a large part of the African continent. That is the reality.

So although I wasn't necessarily going to speak, for that reason and, after listening to you, I decided to propose this plan. Concretely: Cuba offers the United Nations, the World Health Organization and the African countries, the personnel necessary for developing not only AIDS programs but other health care programs as well, and also to give hands-on training to technical and nursing personnel.

The first thing we do in the places we go to is to create a medical school. Africa needs thousands of doctors in order to provide one doctor per 5,000 inhabitants; our country has one doctor per 168 inhabitants. We have experience in health care: currently some 2,000 Cuban doctors are working abroad. This is what I wish to propose concretely here, in the spirit of cooperation. Hopefully the European countries and the industrialized countries represented here, will take account of what I am proposing and make the effort to contribute to finding the medications and to reducing their cost.

What is taking place in the world is worse than warfare. In Africa, one million people die from malaria every year while 300 to 500 million people are infected. Moreover, two million people die of AIDS, and for every two who die, four to five are infected. We know there have not been sufficient advances as yet for a vaccine and it's not known when a vaccine is going to materialize. Three million people die of tuberculosis every year.

We are proposing, concretely, a program for Africa. I am not exaggerating in the least and we are not seeking anything for ourselves. Wherever our doctors go they do not talk about religion, or politics, or philosophy. They have been fulfilling missions for years and have earned the greatest respect and acknowledgement from the local populations. I leave this proposition in the hands of this United Nations round table.

4

"We cannot really speak today of a United Nations' system. We do not have a United Nations' system. What we actually have is a system of domination over almost every country in the world..."

The Role of the United Nations in the 21st Century, UN Millennium Summit, New York
September 7, 2000

I still remember the time when the United Nations was founded. It was immediately after a terrible war against Nazism, in which unexpected alliances were formed among forces with disparate ideological tendencies, bent on fighting that terrible evil threatening humanity.

That war claimed 50 million lives. Several of the main countries at war emerged victorious, and in conjunction with other less powerful nations they founded this institution. Even Cuba was there. Cuba, being a semi-colony, was not at all independent. Actually, almost all the other Latin American countries were semi-colonies, and the majority of countries present here today were not independent either.

Now, we are living a completely new situation. We cannot really speak today of a United Nations' system. We do not have a United Nations' system. What we actually have is a system of domination over almost every country in the world by a small number of powerful nations, which under the aegis of the United States — the most powerful nation of all — decide everything on our planet.

Yesterday I saw a portrait of what the United Nations has become. At lunch there were a number of tables. We plebeians were seated at some of them. There was one table — I watched it closely — where the powerful, who rule the world, were seated. I mean political rule because it cannot be said that all of them rule in economic terms.

Also at the table was a smaller group of those who dominate the world not only politically but economically as well. As is only logical, that table was chaired by our distinguished friend Mr. Kofi Annan, Secretary General of the United Nations, who was to give a speech. Next to him, as is also logical, sat the president of the United States. To his left was our friend the president of Mali, because they needed to add a bit of color somehow. To the right of President Clinton was the president of France. And immediately next to him, also lending some color, was our friend Obasanjo [former president of Nigeria], an illustrious personality. To the left of the president of Mali was Jiang Zemin, leader of a great country which does not dominate the world economically but does have considerable political power. To the left of Jiang Zemin was the prime minister of the United Kingdom, and a bit closer this way, where I could only see his back, was the president of Russia, which is not a major economic power but is a major political power, and especially a major military power. I make a distinction between a superpower, which can destroy a major power about 12 or 14 times over, and a major power, which can destroy the superpower about six or seven times over. So each of them has more than enough power to destroy one another.

Complex issues could have been discussed at the table, such as the consequences for the whole world of the proposed total missile defense shield. Anyone with a minimum of common sense who has heard the candidates — one advocating a partial shield, the other a total shield — can perceive the consequences of such insanity for the Third World, whose development is a source of concern to us.

Well then, that was a real portrait of our United Nations today. Someone here, I think it was the prime minister of Belize, said that those who have the right to decide whether or not the veto privilege is maintained are those who can veto any agreement reached by all of us and any proposal to the contrary.

The veto amounts to a kind of divine right, an absolute power, beside which Louis XIV pales in comparison. While that historic character may have said, *"L'état, c'est moi,"* ["I am the state,"] anyone at that table who is a permanent member of the Security Council could say, *"Les Nations Unies, c'est moi"* ["I am the United Nations,"] especially the mightiest superpower across all fields.

This is a reality but it will not last forever; it cannot last forever because the political and economic order that currently prevails in the world is simply unsustainable and can only lead to disaster.

Their power is very great, especially that of the superpower, since it is the leading economic power, the leading political power, the leading military power, the leading technological power and the leading scientific power. When the prime minister of Saint Lucia said that his country has two Nobel prize laureates I was close to asking him where they were, because according to the information I have, over the last 10 years the major powers have stolen 19 out of 21 Nobel prize laureates in physics, 17 out of 24 in medicine, and 13 out of 22 in chemistry. They carry off all of the science prizes. And they do not only take them from the Third World but also from Europe. Since the Inter-American Development Bank was founded 40 years ago, the rich have stolen a million professionals from Latin America and the Caribbean, including our finest minds. They have plundered us of our greatest talents. We have trained them in our modest universities but they have taken away the most talented. One million professionals!

The cost of training one million professionals in the United States — I did the calculations a while ago — would be around $200 billion. That does not include the cost of senior and junior high school and primary education. They have even stolen our minds. What instruments of domination do they use? Instruments of modern technology.

I wanted to talk a bit about the economic situation, not just the social and human situation. I think I had a figure here somewhere about how the developed nations control 97 percent of the world's patents. They have all of the money in the world as a result of the system established after the last war. Everyone is familiar with the conflict between the ideas of Keynes, from England, and White, the head of the U.S. delegation to Bretton Woods.

Some had conceived of a more logical economic system. The United States controlled 80 percent of the world's gold at that time. A monetary system emerged from Bretton Woods that gave all powers to the United States. Later came the total and absolute veto power in the IMF and the World Bank, another major instrument of economic power for the United States, which is the only country with veto power.

An economic system has been established allowing the United States to control everything new that is created. The WTO, the plan for a Multilateral Agreement on Investments (something they tried to smuggle in) and many other institutions lead to the total dispossession of our prerogatives in every field.

May all tariffs be removed so that Tom Thumb can compete with Gulliver in production, technology and everything else. Our countries really have no chance. I find it very encouraging that we are growing aware of this. I think it is necessary to build an awareness, and to speak clearly about it. Every time we can communicate a message, we should do it, through the media. Although they are in control of the world's leading media, we, the poor, have other ways of getting our messages across. In our battle against the blockade and other things, we can get our message across by satellite to many universities in this country. And through the internet, we can reach every corner of the world. Yesterday we listened to a television program, a round table discussion, over the internet. There are means and ways. I think, however, the best way of building awareness lies in understanding each others' opinions, which have been expressed this afternoon.

After that, there is crisis. I do not recall any time in history when major problems have not been solved through major crises, and the current world order is leading to a tremendous crisis.

There is no longer a real economy. There is a virtual economy. World exports total somewhere over $6 trillion a year. Everyone knows, however, that $1.5 trillion is involved in currency speculation operations, following the elimination of the gold standard in 1971, precisely at the time when the U.S. gold reserves had dropped from an initial $30 billion to just $10 billion. With those $30 billion, it had been able to maintain stability buying gold in times of surplus and selling gold when there was a deficit.

Everyone knows that, but in 1971, after so many hundreds of

billions of tax free dollars had been spent in the Vietnam War, Nixon simply made the unilateral decision, without consulting anyone, to eliminate the gold standard for the U.S. dollar. This led to instability in all currencies. De Gaulle was opposed, of course, because he knew what would follow: the unleashing of speculation. Today, $1.5 trillion is involved in currency speculation every day, in addition to another $1.5 trillion in all sorts of stocks and shares speculation. This has absolutely nothing to do with a real economy.

For example, some stock markets have turned $1,000 into $800,000 in a period of just eight years. It is more of a perception, something in the realm of imagination, based on prospects, even if the companies involved register losses. A colossal virtual economy has been created. An enormous bubble has been inflated and one day it will burst. This is absolutely inevitable. Then, we will be faced with the major crisis that might help to create a new world political and economic order.

Meanwhile, we can build awareness, delve more deeply into these problems and spread ideas like all those that have been expressed here. Everything that has been said here and many other ideas should be disseminated. We cannot be pessimistic. I am convinced that this will happen within a fairly short period of time. We know of everything being planned to bring about world division in the next century. The two U.S. presidential candidates have said that this will be the "American century" for Latin America.

Disputes are cropping up not only with Third World countries but also with Europe, due to conflicts of interest. Somebody very wisely pointed out today that globalization began centuries ago with the division of the world. Before World War I, there was a major expansion of foreign investment. Today, there is a new kind of globalization, supported by what's happening in communications and other fields.

It is my conviction that a crisis is coming. There has been a kind of rebellion here today. At least this assembly has allowed us to freely express ourselves and to say what we believe. I am sure that an ever greater number of people will begin to dare to say what they think, despite their dependence on the World Bank, the IMF and one kind of credit or another. It is our privilege to be able to speak with absolute freedom because we depend neither on the IMF nor the World Bank. For 10 years we have had to endure a double blockade — when the

Soviet Union collapsed we were left doubly blockaded — and we have withstood, thanks to the work carried out by the revolution throughout 40 years and because our country and our people have a sound political consciousness and a great spirit of solidarity.

I feel that this meeting will be very useful, many people have met and spoken and exchanged ideas. At this round table, the most painful things have been said. I will leave with the impression that everyone here has been able to speak. None of the powerful sitting at that table at lunchtime yesterday has been present here. Those of us here are notably the smallest countries, the plebeians, along with a few large countries, like India. The ones who suffer most have been here and we have been able to talk freely. I think this is highly positive.

I will continue to reflect on these matters. For me this meeting has been extremely encouraging, because I can see that our consciousness is growing. With this consciousness we can pressure and struggle. They cannot ignore us when we speak the truth. When a crisis erupts, we will be prepared for a change in these institutions, as we have to be prepared for a change in the political and economic order that currently prevails in the world.

5

"We truly are beginning a millennium that is full of uncertainties."

Riverside Church, Harlem
September 8, 2000

When you asked a few questions about what we have done for our children and our people and the efforts we have made for other children and other peoples in the world, something occurred to me. I thought, all of this has actually had a name — they have called it the "violation of human rights" and used it in an attempt to justify an economic war against Cuba that has lasted more than 40 years.

On my way here, I recalled my four visits to the United Nations. The first time, I was thrown out of the hotel near the United Nations. I had two choices: pitching a tent in the UN courtyard — and as a guerrilla fighter who had recently come down from the mountains, it would not have been all that difficult for me — or heading for Harlem, where I had been invited to stay in one of its hotels. I immediately decided: "I will go to Harlem because that's where my best friends are."

[Someone in the audience shouts, "My house is your house!"]

Thank you very much. That is actually what they used to say to me in the many beautiful homes of the very wealthy people. They had those little signs reading exactly that. Later, when we did some things to help the poor they quickly removed the signs. In you, however, I can sense the generosity of the humble.

All I remember about when I came back the second time, in 1979, is that I spoke on behalf of all the poor countries of the world. The third time, I came back not only to Harlem, but also to the Bronx, as someone said here tonight. This time I have been honored with an invitation to this neighborhood, I believe it is called Riverside. Is that right? From what I can understand, I am beside a river; but at the same time, I am in the middle of a river, a river of the purest and loftiest friendship.

I am sure you can understand that it is not easy for me to visit New York, there is more than enough proof of that. This time it was definitely not easy, and many of my compatriots were very worried. We are living in a special period, and I do not mean the "special period" in Cuba, which has been brought about by the double blockade [of the United States and the collapse of the Soviet Union], but rather the special period of presidential elections. I have received all kinds of threats, from being killed to being sent to a U.S. prison.

However, it was a very important meeting. They called it the Millennium Summit, and we truly are beginning a millennium that is full of uncertainties. What's more, for those of us who believe that the 20th century ends on December 31 [2000], humanity is about to enter the 21st century in extremely difficult and troubling conditions. I could not fail to attend, not for any reason and believe me, after the complicated procedures necessary to obtain a visa, I felt very happy when I got on the plane.

Why did I say that, in my view, the summit was very important? Because the world is suffering a truly catastrophic situation. Do not believe the experts who feign optimism, or those who ignore what is really happening in the world. I have irrefutable statistics about the situation in the Third World, in countries where many of you come from, or countries that have been visited by many U.S. citizens, where three-quarters of humanity live. I have brought a few papers along and chosen various statistics, which I will read.

In the Third World, there are 1.3 billion poor people. In other words, one out of every three inhabitants lives in poverty. More than 820 million people in the world suffer from hunger, and 790 million of them live in the Third World. At the moment of birth, an inhabitant of the Third World can expect to live 18 years less than another of the industrialized world. It is estimated that 654 million people living in countries of the South today will not live past 40 — almost half my age. A full 99.5 percent of all maternal deaths take place in the Third World. The risk of maternal death in Europe is one per 1,400 births. In Africa the risk is one in 16. The number of mothers who die in Africa for every 10,000 births is more than 100 times higher than the number in Europe.

More than 11 million boys and girls under five years of age die every year in the Third World, from diseases that are largely preventable. That means more than 30,000 die every day, 21 every minute, and almost a thousand since this rally began, about 45 minutes ago. Two out of every five children in the Third World suffer from retarded growth, and one in every three is underweight for their age.

In the Third World, 64 children out of every 1,000 live births before reaching one year of age. This figure is an average for all the Third World countries, including Cuba whose infant mortality rate is slightly under seven. There are numerous countries in Africa where more than 200 children out of every 1,000 live births die every year before the age of five. Ten of the 11 new HIV positive cases occurring in the world every minute take place in sub-Saharan Africa, where the total number of people infected is now over 25 million.

All of this is happening at a time when, throughout the world, $800 billion is put into military spending, $400 billion is spent on narcotic drugs, and $1 trillion is invested in commercial advertising.

By the end of 1998, the Third World's external debt amounted to $2.4 trillion. That is four times the total in 1982, only 18 years ago. Between 1982 and 1998, these countries paid over $3.4 trillion for debt servicing, in other words, almost a trillion dollars more than the current debt. Far from decreasing, the debt grew by 45 percent in those 16 years.

Despite neoliberal discourse on the opportunities created by the open-trading system, the underdeveloped countries, with 85 percent of the world's population, accounted for only 34.6 percent of world exports in 1998. That is less than in 1953, despite the fact that since then their population has more than doubled. While the flow of official development assistance in 1992 represented 0.33 percent of the developed countries' gross national product, by 1998, that percentage had dropped to 0.23 percent, far below the 0.7 percent increase goal set by the United Nations. While the wealthy world is becoming increasingly wealthy, contributions to the development of the large number of poor people decrease every year. Solidarity and responsibility shrink further by the year.

On the other hand, the daily volume of currency buying and selling has reached a sum of approximately $1.5 trillion. This figure does not include operations involving so-called financial derivatives, which account for an almost equal additional sum. That is, some $3 trillion worth of speculative operations are carried out every day. If a one percent tax was to be charged on all speculative operations, the amount raised would be more than enough for sustainable development in the so-called developing countries, with the necessary protection of nature and the environment. Actually, these countries are headed down the path of growing and visible underdevelopment, since the gap between the rich and the poor countries is wider every day, as is the difference between the rich and the poor within countries.

I could ask you, for example, whether adding up the savings that all of you may have in the bank, big or small, would amount to even a thousandth of the wealth of the richest man in the world who, by the way, happens to be a citizen of this country.

When the stock markets were created, the phenomena I have described did not exist. This is something totally new, and genuinely absurd. Speculative operations, in which money is used to make money, have absolutely nothing to do with the creation of material goods or services. This is a phenomenon that has developed uncontrollably over the last 30 years and is growing to ever more absurd heights every day. Can this frantic gambling be called economy? Can a genuine economy, trying to meet the vital needs of humankind, withstand it?

Money is no longer invested primarily in the production of goods. It is invested in currencies, stocks and financial derivatives, in a desperate pursuit of more money, through the most sophisticated computers and software and not through productive processes as has historically been the case. This is what the much trumpeted process of neoliberal globalization has brought about. Barely one percent of the $56 billion invested every year in medical research is spent on research into pneumonia, diarrheic diseases, tuberculosis and malaria, four of the primary scourges of the underdeveloped world.

The most advanced medicine used to treat those faced with the tragedy of being HIV positive, costs $10,000 in the industrialized nations. Actual production costs are approximately $1,000.

One of our most sacred principles is that of solidarity, so we are well aware of the tragedies facing the world. Those who do not believe in humankind, in its potential for noble sentiments, in its capacity for goodness and altruism, will never understand that we do not only hurt just for every Cuban child who suffers or dies but also for every child in Haiti, Guatemala, the Dominican Republic, Puerto Rico, Africa and every country in the world. It cannot be claimed that the human species has attained a maximum of consciousness while it is incapable of feeling the suffering of others.

Humanity will attain its greatest consciousness and potential qualities when people feel the same sorrow for the death of any family's child as they would for their own child or other close relative.

I know that many of you — perhaps the vast majority — are Christians, and we are gathered together in a church. Well then, this is exactly what Christ preached. This is what "Love thy neighbor" means to us. This explains the efforts that Cuba has made for other countries, to the extent of its capabilities.

There is a statistic to demonstrate this spirit of solidarity: half a million of our compatriots have carried out internationalist missions in numerous countries in different parts of the world, especially in Africa. They have been medical doctors, teachers, technicians, construction workers, soldiers and others. When many were investing in and trading with the racist and fascist South Africa, tens of thousands of voluntary soldiers from Cuba fought against the racist and fascist soldiers. Today, everyone speaks glowingly of the preservation of Angola's independence, even though the country is still subjected to a brutal civil war. Fault lies with those who supplied the bandits with arms for many years, among them, the apartheid government and other authorities I will not name out of respect for where I am right now. The half a million volunteers who carried out their mission for free did not go there to invest in oil, diamonds, minerals or in any of the country's other riches. Cuba does not have a single investment in any of the countries where our internationalists fulfilled their duty; it does not have a single dollar of capital invested, and it does not own a single square meter of land.

Amílcar Cabral, a great African leader, once made a prophetic statement that was also an unforgettable honor: "When the Cuban soldiers go home, all they will take with them are the remains of their dead comrades." Nobody blockaded the hateful apartheid regime. Nobody waged economic warfare against it. There were no Torricelli or Helms-Burton Acts against that fascist and racist regime. Yet, all these laws and measures have been adopted against Cuba, a country that always has and always will be dedicated to solidarity.

Simply by reducing infant mortality in our country from approximately 60 deaths per 1,000 live births in the first year of life to less than seven per 1,000, we have saved the lives of hundreds of thousands of children. We have protected the health of all children free of charge, and guaranteed a life expectancy of over 75 years. Moreover, we have not only preserved lives but also guaranteed free education for all, and not a selfish and mediocre education but one based on solidarity and excellence. A study carried out by UNESCO revealed that our children possess almost twice as much knowledge as the average child in the rest of Latin America.

We have also saved the lives of hundreds of thousands of children in Africa and other parts of the Third World throughout the years of the revolution, and we have provided health care for tens of millions of people. Over 25,000 health care workers have taken part in these internationalist efforts. They call this the "violation of human rights," and it is why we must be destroyed.

Our revolution has a history. I would have absolutely no moral right to be speaking here if a single Cuban had been murdered by the revolution at some point throughout these 40-plus years; if there were a single death squad in Cuba; if a single person in Cuba had been vanished or if a single person in our country had been tortured — mark my words — if a single person had been tortured. The Cuban people are very much aware of this. They are a rebellious people with a very high sense of justice. They would not have forgiven us a single one of the acts I have mentioned and these people have followed the revolution throughout more than 40 years.

Our country has never been subjected to the "economic shock" policies that wipe out hospitals, schools, social security and vital resources for low-income people. We have rejected these neoliberal policies, and not a single one of those measures has ever been used. Measures that we did implement to confront this terribly difficult situation were discussed with all of the people, and not just in our National Assembly.

Almost half of that National Assembly is made up of district delegates who are nominated and elected by the people, with no intervention by our party. The only role played by the party is in guaranteeing the observation of the procedures set forth in our constitution and our laws for the electoral process.

Nobody needs to spend a penny, not a single one. The district candidates campaign together as a group, as do candidates to the National Assembly who are nominated in every municipality, proportionally to the size of each municipality, although every one must have a minimum of two deputies in the National Assembly. These are the procedures we have developed to guarantee democratic principles. As I was telling you, when we adopted measures to confront the difficult situation of the "special period," every measure was discussed at the grass-roots level first of all, with workers, farmers, students and other mass organizations, at thousands of assemblies, and later at the National Assembly. After the measures had been studied by the National Assembly, they were sent back to the grass-roots level for further discussion before their final adoption by the Assembly.

These measures protected everyone and guaranteed social security for all. Among the main measures adopted were taxes on alcohol, cigarettes and other sumptuary items. Medicines, food and other essential products were never taxed and despite everything, we could still ensure a liter of milk a day for every child up to the age of seven. Do you know how much the population had to pay for that liter of milk? According to the official exchange rate: only 1.5 cents of a U.S. dollar. We still have ration cards and will maintain them for a number of foodstuffs. But a pound of rice, which costs between 12 and 15 cents on the world market — without including transportation costs, since we cannot buy it from the country closest to us, and without including the cost of internal transport and distribution and the rest — is sold to consumers for just under 1.5

cents. A pound of beans is sold for the same price as a liter of milk, 1.5 cents. In our country, the vast majority of citizens pay zero cents of a dollar for the homes they live in, because today, as a result of the revolutionary laws, over 85 percent of homes are owned by the families who live in them. They do not even pay taxes on them. In the remaining homes, located in out-of-the-way places deemed essential for industry or services, tenants pay an extremely low rent or are granted usufruct of them. So when people say that someone earns $15 or $20 a month in Cuba, I say that you have to add the amount for what they would have to pay for housing if they lived in New York, the amount for the cost of education, another certain number of dollars for health care, and other rising costs. I am not saying that we're not poor, or that we do not have needs; but we have distributed our poverty or resources as fairly as possible.

The prices of basic medicines are the same as they were in 1959, over 40 years ago. In 1959, prices were halved, it was one of the first things the revolution did, and those who are administered these medicines in a hospital do not pay a cent for them. If they need a heart transplant, a liver transplant, other transplants or costly operations or treatments, they do not pay a cent.

The revolution has done this for the people. It is only natural that the United States recognizes that the healthiest young people who migrate to the United States, one way or another, are Cubans. In addition, Cubans have higher qualifications than immigrants from any other country in Latin America or the Caribbean.

Our internationalist spirit has not faltered in the slightest during the "special period." We did have to reduce the number of scholarships for foreign students, whose numbers reached 24,000 in the 1980s. Cuba had the highest number of foreign students per capita, among all countries in the world, and we did not charge them a single cent. There are tens of thousands of professionals and technical workers in Africa who studied and graduated in Cuba. I mention Africa, although there have also been students from many other countries, but they primarily came from the world's poorest continent. Their numbers decreased during this past decade.

We also, inevitably, had to cut back for a few years on our programs to support health care efforts in other countries. But I can now say, with great satisfaction, that today we have more doctors and health care workers providing free services in the Third World than at any previous time. After Hurricane George — I don't know why they named it after one of the forefathers of independence in the United States and its first president — caused great devastation and killed many people, we offered Haiti, the poorest country in our hemisphere, all of the doctors it needed. Then the same thing happened a few weeks later in Central America with Hurricane Mitch, which brought sweeping rains associated with climatic changes. These were particularly destructive because the forests had been cut down to export timber to the wealthy countries. We offered the same thing to the Central American countries as we had done to Haiti, and immediately sent hundreds of doctors and proposed the development of comprehensive health care programs.

We felt it was not simply a matter of sending a number of doctors, helping out for two or three weeks after the hurricane and then leaving, because according to the highest estimates made at the time this hurricane had killed over 30,000 people. Perhaps the actual number of deaths was around 15,000, since many of those who were missing eventually showed up. We already knew that over 40,000 children were dying of preventable diseases every year in Central America, not to mention the number of adults. It is like an ongoing, quiet hurricane, much more devastating than Hurricane Mitch, that kills three times as many children every single year as the number killed by Hurricane Mitch, yet nobody ever talks about it.

The countries of Central America, primarily those who were able to act independently, accepted our doctors. Some countries were prohibited from accepting. The health care programs set up at that time are still in operation. In the most isolated locations of one of these countries, where there are snakes, mosquitoes and no electricity, there are currently about 450 Cuban doctors and health care workers — including a few technicians to operate the equipment and a few specialized nurses.

These programs are working and expanding. We do not provide medicines because we do not have them. The medicines are supplied by the governments of the countries involved and some non-governmental organizations. But our doctors' services are supplied absolutely free of charge.

Today, there are several hundred Cuban doctors in Haiti providing medical care to over four million people. There is a group of Cuban specialists in that country's main hospital and also in other hospitals where there are not enough specialists, treating people from any part of the country who need it.

Obviously, saving lives is not so difficult if you follow the simple strategy of immunization with vaccines that cost a few cents. Of course, the same is true if you apply the kind of health care policies that permit lives to be saved and people to be cured at a minimal cost. The lives of millions of children who die in the Third World could be saved for just pennies.

We offered Central America about 2,000 doctors and Haiti as many doctors as it needed. That was not all we did. Following cuts to our military spending, we founded a medical school in Cuba at what used to be a major military facility: a former defense school. There, about 1,000 Central American young people from distant regions and humble backgrounds are studying medicine. First, they do six months of pre-med studies followed by two years of basic sciences at that same school. They then go on to four years of study in any of our country's 20 medical schools which, combined with the schools of basic sciences, currently accommodate 40,000 students.

The new school I have described now has over 3,000 students. In a few months, when the new school year begins, new students will enter the pre-med course. By March, another group of 1,700 students will join bringing the total enrollment to approximately 5,000 students. In three years there will be over 8,000 Latin American medical students, who do not have to pay for their studies and are provided with better food than the 40,000 Cuban university students on scholarships. This is a full program called the Latin American School of Medical Sciences, and it includes all the medical schools spread throughout the country.

Our country has done this in spite of the blockade and at absolutely no cost to the students, who are provided with adequate food and living quarters, laboratory equipment, textbooks and clothing. Other costs are covered as well, such as transportation to and from the school. The invitation was extended to students from all over Latin America as a way to promote unity, community and cultural exchange. The school has cultural groups representing each country. Students will leave with considerable knowledge about the other countries of the region. Above all, the idea is to create a new concept, a new idea about the role of doctors in society — because in the capitals and other big cities of Latin America, there are more than enough doctors, but they have not all been educated about the real duties of a doctor. The number of students is not as important as the ideas that guide this program.

You cannot imagine how eagerly these students apply themselves to their studies or how dedicated they are, even more so than our own students, who are as used to having these opportunities as they are to seeing the sun rise. The Latin American students come from very poor regions where studying medicine was only a dream. The results have been excellent. These schools will turn out excellent doctors! The efforts they are putting into their studies are more than enough compensation for us.

What are we doing in Africa? It would be impossible to bring tens of thousands of Africans to Cuba. You see, even to have one doctor for every 4,000 people, Africa would need a further 160,000 doctors. In order for sub-Saharan Africa to have one doctor for 1,000 people, there would have to be approximately 596,000 doctors. How are they going to train them? There is one solution we have implemented through the Comprehensive Health Care Programs for Africa. We have 3,000 doctors available for sub-Saharan Africa. Their first task is to open medical schools wherever they are needed. They do this by inviting high school graduates and offering a six-month upgrading course. We have just done this in Gambia, where 158 Cuban doctors are working. They asked us for 90 more doctors, which we provided. This was the first country in Africa where our Comrehensive Health Care Program was initiated. Before, they had 30 Gambian doctors for a population of 1.2 million people.

The second country was Equatorial Guinea, where over 100 Cuban doctors are already working and have established a medical school. We had established a medical school in Guinea-Bissau many years ago, but it was destroyed in the civil war supported by foreign intervention. They have not been able to rebuild it yet, and so they asked us if their fifth and sixth year students could continue their studies in Cuba. They were immediately admitted. Because the rebuilding of the school has been delayed, they asked us a few weeks ago if we could take the first, second, third and fourth year students as well. We said, "Send them over right away." Now, all of these students will be able to continue their studies. This is how we work.

There is a massive need to train hundreds of thousands of African doctors and nobody cares to do anything about it. The wealthy countries of the world are only interested in oil, diamonds, minerals, forests, natural gas, cheap labor, and nothing else. As a result, the situation in Africa is much worse today than it was in colonial times, much worse! The population has grown many times over. The situation is dreadful.

I will explain. We have offered all the Caribbean countries free university scholarships, for all those who apply in any field of study. There are many countries in the Caribbean but the total population is not large. They speak English. Why have I spent so much time on the subject of medicine? I recently learned something that really amazed me. We were visited by some members of the Congressional Black Caucus — this is the first time I've discussed it publicly — and as I was telling a Congressperson from Mississippi about these programs he said: "Listen, there are a lot of places in my district where there isn't a single doctor."

"What!" I said. "Ah, now I see: you people are the Third World of the United States." And I said, "We are prepared to send you a few doctors free of charge, the same as we do for other countries of the Third World." I suddenly realized the way things really are. You always hear about how wealthy the United States is, about its gross domestic product of over $8 trillion dollars, and so on. Yet suddenly, there I was talking to a respected member of the U.S. House of Representatives, who was saying that there were not enough doctors in his district. That's why I said, "We can send doctors." Remembering the schools, I immediately added, "There is something more: We are prepared to grant a number of scholarships to poor youth in your district who cannot afford to pay the $200,000 it costs to get a university degree." When they got back to the United States they discussed the matter. They have told us they are studying the question of scholarships, because there are always problems of compatibility among the professional training systems in different countries.

I assured them that our doctors have excellent training. They begin to have contact with community doctors and polyclinics from the very first year, and their six years of medical school include theoretical studies and practical experience. They are constantly in contact with hospitals. Our medical schools were built near the country's most important hospitals in every province. They do their internships and study their areas of expertise right there, so they do not need to leave the provinces to study in the country's capital.

The member of the U.S. House of Representatives said to me that other minorities face the same situation. He told me about the Chicanos, about the Indian reservations and about other parts of the country, and he meant not only Latinos and immigrants but also people born in the United States. I said, "Your country is very big, and we would not be able to do what we do in other countries. I do not know how many people there are living in your Third World, but I imagine there must be about 30 or 40 million."

Do you want to hear something? We have enough doctors for quite a few million people, but I did not dare to offer more because we have a lot of commitments. I said, "This will not solve your huge problem but I am sure that if you need doctors and request visas for these doctors to go there, the authorities could not possibly turn them down."

Something happened a few weeks ago, as a result of a policy promoting the defection of our doctors working in internationalist missions. We have 108 doctors working in provincial hospitals in Zimbabwe because Zimbabwe does not have enough doctors. The apartheid regime in Rhodesia did not train any black doctors. And so what was once Rhodesia, and is now the independent nation of Zimbabwe, after more than 20 years has many hospitals with no doctors. We spread our doctors around and sent teams of at least eight or 10 to almost every province: specialists in comprehensive general medicine; surgeons; orthopedic specialists; anesthesiologists; X-ray technicians and other technicians to repair equipment.

Two of these doctors defected, evidently taken in by the trillion dollars spent every year on advertising that exalts consumerism. The two headed nowhere else than the offices of the UN High Commissioner for Refugees. Right away, the same characters who fought so hard in Congress to keep Elián in the United States addressed the administration to obtain visas for these two doctors. Nobody gave a thought to the children and sick people they had abandoned, those they were providing medical care for and the lives they were saving. The important thing was the publicity: "We snagged two Cuban doctors!" The same has been done by the Cuban American mafia, which is the name we give to something that should never have been called a [Cuban American National] Foundation since it has become a terrorist organization. Now they are busy trying to do the same in Guatemala, Honduras, Belize, Haiti, Guyana, Paraguay, and in the 13 countries where these programs are currently in operation. Cuba plans to extend these programs to roughly 30 or 40 countries, primarily in Africa; who knows how many talents they will manage to steal!

So I said to the U.S. Congressman who visited me in Cuba: "How will they deny you the visas for our doctors, on what grounds, where is the moral right if at the same time they are doing this kind of thing?" To send these doctors, will we have to resort to using the Cuban Adjustment Act? We call it a murderous law because the privileges that are granted to Cubans are not granted to people from any other country in Latin America or the world, causing thousands of lives to be claimed. It is a means of promoting destabilization, disorder and fodder for anti-Cuban publicity.

This is a serious matter, and of course we would not actually do this. It is my hope that if a group of lawmakers from the Black Caucus or the Hispanic minority or representatives of the Native American community requested a number of doctors, who would not cost the taxpayers or the U.S. Treasury anything, then the U.S. Government would not deny them a visa. I could not see the logic of any other decision.

They will argue about the doctors' training. I am absolutely certain that our doctors could be subjected to a rigorous examination by any fair tribunal, and they would successfully pass any tests needed to carry out this mission honorably.

It is easier for the United States to send medical students to Cuba. They are already working on that and I can say that we are prepared to accept 250 students a year from the Third World of the United States. They will learn Spanish and get to know young people from all over the hemisphere, to whom they will teach all they know about the United States and its culture, while the others teach them about theirs. I have already given a figure of 250 scholarships per year, but for the first pre-med course beginning in March we could offer 500 scholarships in order to include other minorities. We would not choose the candidates, they would be selected by the members of Congress who want to help poor young people in their districts to study medicine, and these young people would commit themselves to going back home after they graduate as doctors.

Now I want to add a few things. I was saying that the health situation in Africa is calamitous. The worst part is that a new plague is threatening to exterminate entire nations on that continent. It is threatening to wipe out the population of sub-Saharan Africa, that is, 596 million people.

This is a very serious issue that I am only addressing after much thought. I do not want to sound alarmist but I can tell you without reading from my papers that of the 35 million people in the world who are HIV positive, 25 million are African. Based on information I have from various sources, but mostly from conversations with the head of the UNAIDS program, I can say that more than two million Africans are dying every year from AIDS and these include, as you might imagine, young people and mothers of childbearing age. For every two that die, five more become infected. Nineteen million have already died, there are 12 million orphans, and it is estimated that in the next 10 years this figure will reach 42 million. There is a long way to go before a vaccine is found.

I wonder, how can a poor Third World country develop, in a situation where 30 percent of the population is infected with AIDS and there is a shortage of doctors, medicines and infrastructure? How can 42 million orphan children be cared for? How can these children be fed when so many people are undernourished and hunger is prevalent in many of these countries? It is very distressing that a high percentage of the 19 million who have died are children infected at birth because, of course, many women are infected.

There was a meeting in Durban, South Africa, a few weeks ago and representatives from African countries and industrialized nations spoke. They said that an effort had to be made to deal with this appalling problem. I said to myself, they have just discovered AIDS in Africa, or at least it seems that they have only just discovered it. They discussed what measures to take, what to do with the companies who manufacture the medicines so as to reduce their cost, and what little bit of money could be given to help. They discussed $1 billion, or $1 billion and something. Very well. But they should know that even if they cut down the price of each treatment that stops or begins to stop the development of the disease, from $10,000 to $1,000, they would still need $25 billion annually. If the treatment cost $5,000 they would need $125 billion, and at the current price they would need $250 billion.

We will have to see how much money they agree on, and how

long it will take them to implement a health program, how many more millions will become infected, how many more millions will die and how many more millions will be added to the number of orphans.

I can assure you that with the cooperation of the industrial nations a basic problem could be solved. I was going to refer to this when I mentioned something that has been raised by several African representatives, who have said: "What is the point? What is the point if we do not have the infrastructure required to use these medicines?" Treatments consist of a cocktail of drugs to be administered at such and such a time and under such and such conditions. They are not aspirins which one takes for a headache.

Yesterday in the United Nations, many African representatives addressed the AIDS issue, and recalling what was discussed in Durban, I said: "If the industrial nations put up the money for the medicines, then our country, thanks to experience acquired through the work of tens of thousands of doctors in the Third World, could set up that infrastructure in one year to fight AIDS and other diseases. Do not worry about politics because our doctors have strict instructions to follow, one rule above all: 'Never discuss politics, religion or philosophy.' And they abide by that rule."

With the progress of such a terrible epidemic, many people will soon be unable to work or produce food and the few hospital beds they have will not be enough because AIDS brings with it other terrible diseases. To this health predicament we should add the hundreds of millions of cases of infection or reinfection with malaria, which kills one million people every year, and the three million who die from tuberculosis, a disease unquestionably linked to malnutrition and HIV. I have already said that only one percent of total world spending on health research programs is used to research tropical diseases. The infrastructure could also be useful in providing other medical services, not only medication for AIDS. If there are medicines and vaccines to treat or prevent other diseases which affect many people, these could be fought as well. Services could be provided which are indeed fairly economical. We could send a minimum of 100 doctors to each of the countries in most need in sub-Saharan Africa.

Those doctors would organize the infrastructure and direct and train the young people. If they were assigned young 15-year-old assistants with sixth-grade educations, with the right books they could turn them into nurses in half the time needed in a nursing school. If they wanted to train orthopedic specialists, surgeons or specialists in other fields of medicine, they could train them in half the time used for a residency in a hospital. Those doctors could do much more than create the infrastructure: they could train tens of thousands of qualified personnel. In addition, they could open university schools of medicine in countries where they do not exist. Cuba would not charge a single cent for those services, or wait years to implement them. They will say that there is no money. Well, a little bit could be taken from the amount spent on advertising, which encourages consumption not only in developed societies but also among billions of people living in underdeveloped countries, where they can hardly consume anything. They could also take a small amount from military spending, which currently totals $800 billion.

They could release a worldwide issue of bonds and many good people could buy bonds as part of their contribution. With a small tax on speculative operations there would be more than enough money, and not just for this but practically enough to develop the whole Third World. It is necessary, it is absolutely crucial.

Why has it not been done? Why do they talk so much about human rights when all these catastrophic things are happening in the world? Who is responsible for the deaths of tens of millions of people every year whose lives could be saved? There are 11 million children among that number — as well as teenagers, young people and adults, who also die for lack of treatment or of some malformation that could have been repaired, or because they needed surgery or an orthopedic operation after an accident. It is not known how many die who could be saved, or how many old people could live a little longer.

A person who lives 50 years — you know a lot of them and have many relatives like that — would like to live 10 more years, 20 or 30 more years. And 70 year olds would like to live five, eight or 10 more years. People my age, 74, as you remembered today, would like to live four or five or even 10 more years to see how the world evolves and if any predictions come true.

Ethics and honorable behavior are invaluable. They are the most powerful force anyone can have.

I have told you about my trips and about all the threats. I even said I would like to live a few years more. Nevertheless, I can assure you that in exchange for my life I would not change a single principle, I would not accept a single dishonor, I would not give in to a single threat. I told you I was happy when I began the trip to this country, to New York rather, as I do not have a visa to visit the country, only for New York and within 25 miles, not a millimeter beyond. I was pleased of my desire to meet with you and my contempt for the series of threats.

Perhaps these views I have offered you will be useful for others who, like you, have been so brave and have shown us so much solidarity. I have spoken of the Third World's serious social problems. There are serious social problems even in such a rich country as this one, the richest country in the world. I want to mention some of them. Thirty-six million people, 14 percent of the population, live below the poverty line, a rate twice as high as that of other developed countries — double that of Europe and Japan. Forty-three million people do not have health cover and another 30 million have such low medical coverage that it is practically nonexistent.

There are 30 million illiterates and another 30 million functional illiterates. Cuba did not make this up, these are official figures from international organizations.

Among the black population the rate of poverty is over 29 percent; the rate for the whole population is 14 percent. The poverty rate among the black population is more than twice that of the general population of the United States. Among black children the figure reaches 40 percent. In some cities and rural areas in the United States it is over 50 percent.

Despite economic expansion, the poverty rates in the United States are two to three times higher than those in Western Europe, and 22 percent of U.S. children live in poverty. These are official figures.

Only 45 percent of all workers in the private sector have social security coverage. It is estimated that 13 percent of the total U.S. population will not live beyond 60 years of age. Women still earn only 73 percent of what men earn in comparable jobs and make up 70 percent of part-time workers, those who have no right to any social benefits. Between 1981 and 1995, 85 percent of new workers with more than one job were women.

The richest one percent of the population, who in 1975 owned 20 percent of the wealth, now owns 36 percent. The gap keeps widening. There is not one millionaire, not one person who belongs to the upper middle class, among the 3,600 people sentenced to capital punishment who are now on death row in U.S. prisons. One might wonder why. You perhaps have a better answer than I do. I am not accusing anyone, I'm simply saying what goes on.

Apparently, one needs to reach the category of millionaire to have the decency and discipline needed never to be targeted for such a sentence. There are more statistics, which are a little hard to take, but which I have to tell you about.

It is an historical fact, that during the time rape was considered a capital crime, 405 of the 455 people executed for rape were black: that is to say, nine out of 10. In the state of Pennsylvania, for example, where the Declaration of Independence was proclaimed in 1776, only nine percent of the total population is black. Yet, 62 percent of those sentenced to death are black — that is a proportion seven times greater than the total population.

One more thing, more than 90 percent of the 3,600 people sentenced to death were victims of physical or sexual abuse during their childhood. A recent study by a nongovernmental organization indicates that when it comes to drug-related offenses, black males are 13 times more likely to be given longer sentences than white males, although there are five times as many white males dealing drugs in the United States. More than 60 percent of the women in prison in the United States are African American or Hispanic.

Perhaps all of us Hispanics, African Americans, and people from different ethnic groups are particularly prone to committing all sorts of crimes.

I am not glossing over the crimes that may have been committed, far from it. Neither am I in a position to accurately know what the procedures are like here, and what usually happens. I simply wonder why. If we are genetically criminal, it would not matter if all of sub-Saharan Africa, if all the indigenous peoples, if all the mixed race people and all the white people in Latin America, if all the people in the Caribbean nations including Cubans, of course, were disappeared. This is a question that we have at least the right to ask ourselves.

I will add a few words to what I have said so far. You mentioned a while ago the name of an African American recently executed. You know that our people vigorously condemned the judicial murder of Shaka Sankofa for a crime he did not commit. The execution occurred despite unanimous condemnation from world public opinion and even from many governments in the world.

I requested a lot of information. I went as far as looking at small maps and sketches of the place where the crimes he was accused of were committed. Only one person claimed to have seen him, at night, from quite a distance, a quick glance that not even the most sensitive camera could have recorded. That, and other evidence, led me to believe in his innocence. Not because someone claimed it was true, but because I analyzed all the information and reached that conclusion. I analyzed his social origins, the marginality into which he was born, his first clashes with the law. When talking to our own people, I have quoted these as examples of the true factors that lead a young man, black or white or of whatever ethnic group, to commit a crime. Also, I am a lawyer. I know something about law. I defended myself when I was on trial for the attack on the Moncada garrison and I have had to do so more than once since I became a lawyer. I hardly had any other clients!

I am equally well aware that for some time now you have been caught up in a very just struggle, a struggle that our people also fully support: the struggle for the release of Mumia Abu-Jamal, a journalist sentenced to death whose unfair trial has given rise to a giant protest movement throughout the world.

If we go a bit further and analyze the historical data, that one white man for every nine African Americans has been executed for rape, we see that other factors aside, the element of social marginality has always been present. As is the case with the African Americans, racial discrimination is added to social marginality, and tens of millions of people suffer horribly from this injustice, including those who have never been sentenced to death or to prison. They were born sentenced to humiliation every day of their lives.

I went to the United States for a few days in 1956, I think. I was living in Mexico, preparing to go back to Cuba. I visited New York and other places to meet with the few Cuban immigrants that were in the United States, at a time when the Cuban Adjustment Act did not exist. One could not just arrive on a boat or raft; there were almost no Cuban immigrants here back then. It was actually the Cuban Revolution that opened the doors for hundreds of thousands of people who had wanted to emigrate for a long time, but had no hope of doing so.

We could remind those who so hate Cuba, the revolution and myself, in particular, that they should thank the revolution every now and then, because without it there would not be many Cuban millionaires, there would be no so-called Cuban American National Foundation, there would be no Cuban members of the U.S. Congress, they would not be able to sponsor certain bills, they would not be courted in election campaigns, they would not be granted their every wish (even though a large majority of them do not vote, because given the privileges granted them, it suits them to be Cuban rather than U.S. citizens).

How many resident's visas were granted in the 30 years before the triumph of the revolution? An insignificant number in the 1930s and 1940s, and scarcely 2,000 or 3,000 between 1950 and 1959.

It is well known that in the first few days of January 1959, a large number of war criminals, embezzlers and accomplices of Batista who had murdered thousands of Cubans and looted the country, found safe haven in the United States. The first revolutionary laws that had to do with recovering embezzled goods, lowering the rates for basic services, giving back employment to workers unjustly dismissed during the [Batista] dictatorship, urban and agrarian reforms and other measures of elementary social justice, terrified the richest sectors of our society and they began to emigrate to the United States.

From the first day of the revolution, visas for the United States were unusually easy to obtain, especially for those from the upper and middle classes, for doctors and other university educated professionals, professors, teachers, technicians and skilled workers. Many of these people had always longed to immigrate to this country. Hostility toward the revolution, and the aim of depriving us of a skilled labor force were obvious motivations almost immediately. They also needed some of Batista's former officers and young people to feed the mercenary brigade [to invade Cuba], a plan that nobody knew about at that time. Permission was always given by the Cuban Government to those leaving legally for the United States.

Even during the fighting at the [1961] Bay of Pigs, commercial air flights were not interrupted. After the [1962] Missile Crisis the U.S. abruptly suspended the flights and the visas. Tens of thousands of families were separated. On the other hand, even before the Cuban Adjustment Act, they allowed anyone who reached their shores by any means available to them — even by hijacking planes or boats — to enter U.S. territory.

After the [1965] Camarioca incident, 360,000 Cubans left the country legally, in absolute safety and without a single victim. Among these, in addition to relatives of U.S. residents, there were large numbers of professionals and teachers who could earn a salary 10 times higher in the United States than in Cuba, and skilled workers and technicians from major industries. They were in fact economic migrants. Nevertheless, everyone who went to the United States was given the name of "political refugee" or "exile." If this concept were applied to Mexicans and other Latin Americans who migrate to the United States, there would be between 12 and 15 million Mexican political refugees, a million Haitian political refugees, a million Dominican political refugees, hundreds of thousands of Central American political refugees, and who knows how many Puerto Rican political refugees. Puerto Ricans are patriots and love their country, so why do they come to the United States? For economic reasons, and there are almost as many here in the United States as there are on the island.

One million Puerto Ricans live in New York. We saw them supporting the just cause of Vieques this year. In Cuba, we televised a round table discussion on the subject.

These round tables are fed directly to the internet in English, of course, the language most spoken throughout the world. Unfortunately only one percent of Africans have access to the internet, so we must reach them by radio. The same thing applies in Latin America.

Speaking of communications and cooperation with Third World countries, I want to inform you that we have developed a program to teach reading and writing by radio. This idea came up one day when I asked the president of Niger, who was visiting Cuba, what the illiteracy rate was in his country. He mentioned an 87 percent illiteracy rate, where only 17 percent of the population have any schooling. We are celebrating the arrival of the new century and the new millennium yet we still have to wonder: In what century of the third millennium, will that country with the same population as Cuba, have eradicated illiteracy? I asked the president, "Do they have radios?" He said, "Yes, almost every family has a radio."

I suggested to a group of Cuban educational experts that they study the possibility of teaching reading and writing by radio, by developing a small manual which, using pictures of animals, plants and common objects would identify the letters of the alphabet and make it possible to learn syllables, words and phrases, and to introduce concepts in the given language, using radio broadcasts under the guidance of specialized teachers. In three months, our educational experts designed a method which, when tested in the Creole language in Haiti with 300 illiterate people, showed really promising results. A literacy course using television would be very simple, but access to television is difficult for the majority of the world's illiterates. Our educational specialists, who created and monitored the experiment are astounded. The course is ready in French, Portuguese and Creole.

It is another way of cooperating with the Third World, by teaching hundreds of millions of people to read and write, for an infinitesimal cost. It is hard to imagine how humiliated a person feels when they cannot read and write. I am reminded of my mother and my father, who barely knew how to read and write, and I can bear witness to how much they suffered. I know they did. That suffering explains the hunger for knowledge that exists in our country.

I think that our country is on its way to a completely new era. I am not claiming that our country is a perfect model of equality and justice. We believed, at the beginning, that when we had established full equality before the law and complete intolerance of sexual discrimination in the case of women, or racial discrimination in the case of ethnic minorities, these phenomena would vanish from our society. It was some time before we discovered that marginality and racial discrimination are not things that one gets rid of with a law or even with 10 laws, and we have not managed to eliminate them completely, even in 40 years.

There has never been and there never will be a case where the law is applied according to ethnic criteria. We did discover, however, that the descendents of slaves who had lived in the slave quarters were the poorest, and continued to live, after the supposed abolition of slavery, in the poorest housing.

There are marginal neighborhoods; there are hundreds of thousands of people who live in marginal neighborhoods, and not only blacks and mixed race people, but whites as well. There are marginal whites, too, and all this we inherited from the previous social system. Our country is on its way to a new era. I hope someday to be able to speak to you of the things we are doing today and how we will continue to do them.

We do not have the money to build housing for all the people who live in what we could call marginal conditions. But we have lots of other ideas which need not wait and which our united and justice loving people will implement to get rid of even the tiniest vestiges of marginality and discrimination. I have faith that we will succeed, it is the endeavor of the leaders of our youth, our students and our people.

We are aware there is still marginality in our country. But there is the will to eradicate it with the proper methods for this task to bring more unity and equality to our society. On behalf of my homeland, I promise to keep you informed about the progress of our efforts.

When those U.S. friends went to Cuba and talked to us of the two cases I mentioned, Sankofa and Mumia, they supplied me with detailed information about their lives and the injustices committed against them. The televised round tables helped to spread awareness about the seriousness of what was happening. It is not a disgrace to be poor, the errors that any person might commit as a child or a teenager are not a disgrace. What is a disgrace is that in the century which is just beginning, with all the technological advances that have been made, when humankind even has aspirations to populate the planet Mars, there are children, teenagers and adults living on our planet in conditions of marginality, and that in many countries as well as being marginalized those people are discriminated against.

At this rate, with these models of consumerism that lead to the destruction of the natural means of life, of the atmosphere, to shortages and pollution of drinking water and of the seas, to climatic changes, natural disasters, to poverty, to deeper and widening gaps within countries and between countries, you can state with precision that the social and economic order which exists in the world today is unsustainable. I feel that these are truly important issues.

6

*"The capital outflow [from the Third World] constitutes genocide...
since the toll in material and human losses is higher than in a war.
Is this fair? Is this democratic? Is this humane?"*

National Assembly, Caracas, Venezuela
October 27, 2000

I am not here for protocol reasons or because tradition would have it that official guests visit parliament. I do not belong to that stock of men who run after honors, ask for privileges or live as slaves to conceit. When visiting a country, particularly if it is a beloved sister country such as Venezuela, I respect the wishes of those who represent it with great dignity and courage.

Regrettably, the very idea of my visit to the Venezuelan parliament, included in the itinerary by our hosts, was a source of annoyance to some of its distinguished members. I offer my apologies. It is my duty to be polite but I will equally avoid an excessively refined language, too diplomatic or reeking of affectation. I shall use deliberately clear and sincerely honest words.

It is not my first visit to the Venezuelan parliament; the first time was over 41 years ago. It would not be accurate to say, however, that I have returned to the same institution, or that I am the same man I was then. Closer to the truth is, in fact, that I am a different man coming to a different parliament.

Personally, I have no merits to take credit for or apologies to offer. At that time, I was a 32-year-old inexperienced man who by mere chance had survived many risks. I was simply lucky, and that is not something to take credit for. Usually, human beings have plenty of dreams and ideals although very few enjoy the elusive privilege of seeing them realized. Even if they do, that gives them no right to boast.

That parliament, which I had the honor to meet with so long ago, also had plenty of dreams and hopes. A popular uprising had succeeded months before. Everything has changed since then. Dreams and hopes were reduced to ashes, and on those ashes this parliament and new hopes have been built. Throughout history people have had dreams, a right that will exist forever. The great miracle is that the hopes and dreams of this noble and heroic people may come true.

Like many of you, I also harbor dreams that come from the extra-ordinary events that have occurred in Venezuela at the end of the last four decades. Venezuelans who fought against each other in the past have become revolutionary allies, guerrillas have become outstanding politicians, and soldiers have turned into daring leaders who are raising the banners that once filled this nation with glory.

It is not for me to pass judgment on those who moved from the left to the right, or on many who began as honest conservatives only to end up plundering and deceiving the people. It is neither my purpose, nor can I assume my right, to play judge of the personalities involved in the dramatic experiences you have endured. All people are ephemeral and often erratic, even those who act in good faith. I abide by the right that José Martí bequeathed every Cuban, that is the right to feel an enormous admiration for Venezuela and for the greatest dreamer and statesman in our hemisphere: Simón Bolívar. He conceived of a united, independent and Latin homeland, and he fought for it. He was never in favor of colonialism or the monarchy, not even when the Patriotic Junta was created in rebellion against the imposition of an alien monarch in the Spanish throne.

From adolescence, Bolívar was resolutely on the side of independence, as early as 1805. Half of South America was freed by his sword, and in the historic battle of Ayacucho, with the brave soldiers of Greater Colombia, under the direct command of the immortal General Sucre, he ensured the independence of the rest of South and Central America.

The United States of America was then, as we all know, just a group of recently liberated British colonies enmeshed in an expansionist process. Still, the great Venezuelan leader guessed, at that very early stage, "...they seem destined by Providence to spread calamities in the Americas in the name of freedom."

I understand perfectly the diversity of interests and points of view that inevitably exist in Venezuela today. It has been said that before the Battle of the Pyramids, during his campaign in Egypt, Napoleon Bonaparte addressed his troops: "Soldiers, from the top of these pyramids, 40 centuries are looking upon you."

Greatly honored by the invitation to address this assembly, I would dare say with absolute modesty: Venezuelan brothers and sisters, from this rostrum, 41 years and 10 months of experience in the restless struggle against hostility and aggression, by the mightiest power that has ever existed on earth, look upon you in admiration and share the strenuous battle that you are fighting today, with the inspiration of Simón Bolívar.

Describing relations between our two countries the much-touted argument has been that Venezuela intends to introduce Cuba's revolutionary model. On the eve of the referendum on the new Venezuelan Constitution, there was so much talk about it, that I found myself needing to meet with a group of local journalists who represented major journals, radio stations and TV networks. Those who cynically invoked Cuba as an evil ghost — the way the imperialists depict us in their gross lies — made us feel entitled to hold such a press conference.

In a night with less sleep than I have ever had before, even in my feverish youth as a student, I read and underlined the basic concepts in that draft and compared them with those in our own constitution. Later, holding the Cuban Constitution in one hand and in the other the Venezuelan draft , I pointed out the profound differences between the revolutionary concepts of one and those of the other. I say "revolutionary," because they both are. They both intend to provide a better life for their peoples; they wish for radical changes; they long for justice; their mutual aspiration is to attain a closer unity among the peoples of the Americas. As José Martí said: "There is nothing more that is necessary to say! There is only one people from the Bravo River to the Patagonia." Both countries are steadily fighting for the preservation of their sovereignty, their independence and their cultural identities.

Our constitution is essentially based on the social ownership of the means of production and the planning of development; on the active, organized and massive participation of all the people in political activities and the construction of a new society; on the close unity of all the people under the leadership of a party that looks after norms and principles but that does not nominate or elect representatives to the state bodies, since this is a task carried out fully by the people through their mass organizations and established legal procedures.

The Venezuelan Constitution rests on a market economy scheme where private property is extensively guaranteed. Montesquieu's three famous powers, proclaimed as the main pillars of the traditional bourgeois democracy, are complemented with new bodies and the strength required to preserve the balance in the political leadership of the society. The multiparty system is also set forth as a basic element. Actually, one would have to be really ignorant to find any similarity between the two constitutions.

At the meeting with the Venezuelan media representatives, I denounced the first steps of the terrorist Cuban American mafia in Miami to assassinate the president of Venezuela. The gangsters felt, in a way, that Venezuela could be a new Cuba. I also described the generous flow of funds coming from Miami to pay for the electoral campaign against President Chávez. I offered accurate data and disclosed a few indispensable names. They all denied it, of course. One past government official, reputed as being well-educated and efficient, swore that he was absolutely innocent of the role attributed to him. I avoided reiterating my statement although I had then, and I still have, accurate information about how he received half a million U.S. dollars, who brought that amount to Venezuela and who delivered the money to the final payees. Ultimately, it was not even necessary. Those involved in the conspiracy were crushed by the people's vote on July 30. The information could be kept in reserve in case it became necessary to use it any time in the future.

Cuba is continually being used as an element in Venezuela's domestic politics; they keep trying to use Cuba to attack Chávez, an indisputable and outstanding leader and follower of Bolívar's ideas, whose actions and prestige exceed the boundaries of his homeland. I am his friend and I take pride in it. I admire his courage, his honesty and his clear understanding of the problems in today's world and the extraordinary role that Venezuela has to play in Latin American unity and in the struggles of the Third World countries. I am not saying this now because he is the president of Venezuela; I could guess who he was even as he was in prison. Only a few months after his release I invited him to Cuba, where he was properly welcomed. I introduced him to the university students; he addressed them in the main hall of the University of Havana, and was met with great enthusiasm.

The resounding popular victory he obtained four years later — penniless, lacking the handsome resources of the old political clique whose campaigns were funded with large amounts of money stolen from the people — he gained only with the power of his ideas, his capacity to convey them to the masses and the support of small organizations of Venezuela's most progressive forces. His victory marked the end of his adversaries. A remarkable opportunity was born not only for this country but for our hemisphere as well.

I have never asked anything from Chávez. I have never appealed to him to include my homeland, criminally blockaded for more than four decades, in the San José Pact. On the contrary, I have always offered Cuba's modest cooperation in any area that could be of use to Venezuela. Cuba's inclusion was entirely his idea, and I heard it for the first time when he publicly addressed the issue at a Summit of the Association of Caribbean States, held in the Dominican Republic in April, 1999. There, he expressed his wish that several Caribbean nations, which had not been part of the agreement, be included. His profound identification with Bolívar's thought has inspired him to act as a bridge between Latin America and the principled Caribbean countries.

I am aware that my visit to Venezuela has been the target for all sorts of poisonous campaigns. President Chávez has been accused of wanting to give Cuba oil for free and of using the Caracas Pact as a simple pretext to help Cuba. If this were the case, he would deserve a monument as high as Mount Everest, because Cuba has been isolated, betrayed and blockaded by every government in this hemisphere except Mexico. These governments were subjugated to the United States, including Venezuela's Government, led by its first constitutional president after the popular uprising of January 23, 1958, and the inception of the Patriotic Junta, which headed the elections that same year.

Despite the blockades, dirty war, mercenary invasions and threats of direct attack, our people have honorably defended their homeland in the frontline of the Americas. Martí foresaw this when, on the eve of his death in combat [in 1895], he confessed that everything he had done in his life was "...to prevent the United States from spreading through the Antilles as Cuba gains its independence, and from overpowering with that additional strength our lands of America."

None of those accusing Chávez have ever opposed the efforts to kill the Cuban people by hunger and disease, something that can only be described as genocide. They further seem to forget that when oil prices were exceedingly low and Venezuela's economic situation was critical, it was Chávez who reinvigorated OPEC [Organization of Petroleum-Exporting Countries], whose actions have tripled the prices in less than two years.

It is true that today's prices, perfectly tolerable for the industrial and wealthy nations, are exacting a heavy toll from over 100 Third World countries, while Venezuela's income and those of the other oil producing countries have grown considerably. Chávez tried to compensate for this with the Caracas Pact which, as you know, offers a group of Central American and Caribbean nations the facility to pay part of the price on credit, with low interest rates and on a long term basis. It is a good example that other oil exporting countries would do well to imitate.

Those who oppose this initiative of Chávez, which due to the current high prices involves only a small portion of Venezuela's income, are exhibiting an extremely selfish and shortsighted reaction. They overlook the fact that without the support of the Third World nations, OPEC would be in no position to withstand for long the enormous pressures of the industrial and wealthy countries affected by the increase in the price of gasoline for their billions of cars and other motor vehicles.

What is ignored is that Cuba is rapidly increasing its oil production and that, in a relatively short period, it will be self-reliant in oil and gas. Venezuela's cooperation with Cuba in the area of energy, by providing advanced technology leading to higher levels of extraction and the use of our own petroleum, will indeed be of invaluable assistance. On the other hand, the oil supplied under the conditions of the Caracas Pact, will be rigorously paid for in hard currency as well as in goods and services which will doubtlessly prove of great value to the Venezuelan people.

Our cooperation with Venezuela is inspired by much more transcendental ideals than trade exchange between the two countries. We share a mutual awareness of the need to unite the Latin American and Caribbean nations and to struggle for a world economic order that brings more justice to all peoples. This is no written pact but rather common objectives expressed in our common actions at the United Nations, the Group of 77, the Nonaligned Nations Movement and other relevant international forums.

The common purpose of both countries in the international political arena is eloquently expressed in their rejection of neoliberal policies and their willingness to strive for economic development and social justice. Those so fiercely bent on lying, slandering and conspiring against the exemplary relations between our two countries, who have tried to jeopardize the Cuban delegation's official visit and to distort the meaning of economic cooperation between Cuba and Venezuela, should explain to the Venezuelan people why, in a country with huge economic resources and an industrious and intelligent people, poverty engulfs an incredible 80 percent of the population.

I will limit myself to a few examples. According to sources from ECLA and the Andean Community, the poor sectors, which a decade ago already made up 70 percent of the population, grew eight years later to 77 percent. Levels of absolute poverty climbed from 30 to 38 percent. Meanwhile, unemployment has reached 15.4 percent and precarious employment in the informal sector involves 52 percent of the labor force.

Previous official data showed illiteracy rates at less than 10 percent. Presently, official sources from the Venezuelan Ministry of Education estimate that real illiteracy is affecting 20 percent of the population. Fifty percent of all students drop out of school for economic reasons, 11 percent due to poor school performance and nine percent for lack of opportunities. These figures add up to 70 percent of students.

In the last 21 years, the capital outflow from Venezuela amounted to $100 billion, a real drain of financial resources indispensable for the country's economic and social development. Such information, provided by various sources, is really overwhelming. It would be impossible to cite all the calamities inherited by Chavez's "Bolivarian Revolution," although one should inescapably be mentioned as reflects all the others. It is infant mortality, an extremely sensitive human and social issue.

UNICEF data indicates that in 1998 infant mortality among Venezuelan children under the age of one was 21.4 per 1,000 live births. That figure grew to 25 when children under the age of five were included. How many Venezuelan children could have survived if following the political process initiated in 1959, almost simultaneously with the Cuban Revolution, infant mortality had been reduced in Venezuela at the pace and to the degree that it was reduced in Cuba, from an estimated 60 to 6.8 for the first year of life and from 70 to 8.3 among children under five?

The figures show that in the 40 year period between 1959 and 1999, a total of 365,510 children whose lives could have been saved, died in Venezuela. In Cuba, whose population in 1959 was hardly seven million, the revolution has saved the lives of hundreds of thousands of children by reducing infant mortality rates to levels which today are better than those of the United States of America, the wealthiest and most developed nation in the world. By the age of seven none of these children is illiterate and today, tens of thousands of them have become qualified technicians or university graduates.

In the year 1998 alone, which marked the end of the nefarious stage that preceded the elections, 7,951 children — whose lives could have been saved — died in Venezuela in their first year of life, a figure that grows to 8,833 if children under five are also included. In all cases I quote exact figures officially reported by UN agencies.

The number of Venezuelan children dead in a year is thus higher than the number of soldiers from both sides who fell in the battles of Boyacá, Carabobo, Pichincha, Junín and Ayacucho, five of the most important and decisive battles fought during the independence wars waged by Bolívar. Who killed those children? Which of the culprits was sent to jail? Who was accused of genocide? The tens of billions of dollars embezzled by corrupt politicians constitutes genocide, because the funds they steal from the public coffers cause the deaths of an incalculable number of children, adolescents and adults, who perish from preventable and curable diseases. That truly murderous political and social order — whose people's protests are forcibly suppressed with real bullets and death — is presented to the world public as a model of freedom and democracy.

The capital outflow also constitutes genocide. When the financial resources of a Third World nation are transferred to an industrial nation, its reserves are depleted, its economy stagnates, unemployment and poverty grow, public health and education face the brunt of the blow and that translates into pain and death. I would rather avoid making estimates, since the toll in material and human losses is higher than in a war. Is this fair? Is this democratic? Is this humane?

The face of this model of a social order can be seen in the outskirts of large cities in our hemisphere, which overflow with marginal neighborhoods where dozens of millions of families live in subhuman conditions.

If it were not taken as an interference, I would like to meditate and speak my mind, and I would like to say this: I have always felt that if Venezuela had an efficient and honest administration over the last 40 years, it could have achieved economic development similar to that of Sweden. There is no possible justification for the poverty and social calamity reflected in official Venezuelan reports and in those of international organizations. Actually, those who were leading this country when I first visited parliament created the conditions for the unavoidable emergence of the current revolutionary process. If the new generation of leaders in the country today pool their forces, close ranks and do everything within their capabilities, those who are longing for a return to the lost years will never again win the people's trust. Is it possible to do it within the framework of the recently elaborated, and approved, political and constitutional model? Yes, I think it is.

The immense political and moral authority emanating from what the "Bolivarian Revolution" can do for the people would politically crush the reactionary forces. The revolutionary and patriotic values and culture that it would create among the Venezuelan people would render it impossible to return to the past.

Another perfectly logical but more complex question could also be asked: Can higher levels of justice than presently exist be attained in a market economy? I am a convinced Marxist and a socialist. I think that the market economy produces inequalities, selfishness, consumerism, wastage of resources, and chaos, and that a minimum planning of economic development and the setting of priorities are indispensable. But I also feel that in a country with the huge resources of Venezuela, the "Bolivarian Revolution" could obtain, in half the time, 75 percent of what Cuba — a blockaded country with infinitely fewer resources than Venezuela — has achieved since the victory of the [1959] revolution.

I mean that this government could, in a few years, totally eradicate illiteracy and provide a first class education to all children and adolescents and a high cultural level to most people; ensure excellent medical care to every person; create jobs for young people; strike out embezzlement; reduce criminality to a minimum and provide decent housing to all Venezuelans.

A rational distribution of wealth, through an adequate taxation system, is possible in a market economy. Of course, that demands a total devotion to work by all members of the revolutionary forces. In my view, on a short term basis, Venezuela does not have much choice. It is easily said but this can be an extremely hard and strenuous task. On the other hand, no less than 70 percent of the wealth here is state owned — neoliberalism did not have enough time to give it up to foreign capital — so there is no need for nationalization.

In the period Cuba is going through, but progressively leaving behind, we have learned that a great number of variables are possible in the development of the economy and the solution of problems. It can be done if the state plays its role, putting first the interests of the nation and the people. We have accumulated a great deal of experience in doing a lot with little resources and having a strong political and social impact. There is a solution for every problem and all obstacles can be overcome.

Being absolutely objective, I should say that in Venezuela today there is only one person who can lead such a complex process, and that is Hugo Chávez. His death, either intentional or accidental, would terminate that possibility and bring about chaos. By the way, having come to this point in my life, and as I have come to know him somewhat, I must say that Chávez does not contribute to his own security, since he is reluctant to accept even a minimum of adequate measures. You can help him, and also his friends and his people, persuading him to be more cooperative. You should not have any doubts that his adversaries, both external and domestic, will try to have him physically removed. I say this because I have been through the peculiar experience of being the target of over 600 such [assassination] attempts carried through to various degrees of completion. An Olympic record!

I know that enemy only too well, I know how they think and act. This trip to Venezuela has been no exception. I am aware that once again they have toyed with finding a possible way to carry out their so far thwarted designs. But that is not important. Contrary to the present situation in the Venezuelan process, in Cuba there has always been and forever will be somebody, actually many people, who can take up my work. I am not like Chávez, a young, lively leader with great tasks still to undertake. He should take care of himself.

I have honored my word. I have spoken with absolute honesty, avoiding excessive diplomacy or affectation. I have talked to you as a friend, as a brother, as a Cuban, as a Venezuelan.

7

"Children are more severely affected by poverty. No other age group is as vulnerable since the physical and psychological damage they sustain affects them for life."

The 10ᵗʰ Ibero-American Summit, Panama City
November 17 & 18, 2000

It was a happy initiative to adopt "United for children and adolescents: justice and equality in the new millennium," as the central focus of this summit. That idea alone would suffice to give meaning to this significant gathering.

The situation for children is different in every one of our nations. Despite progress made in the last two decades, partly due to the relevant initiatives and tenacious efforts undertaken by UNICEF, WHO [World Health Organization] and other UN agencies — more or less warmly received and supported by national governments, taking into account disparities in development and resources — life for Latin American children in general is very dramatic.

Forty-five percent of the total population in Latin America and the Caribbean region is poor, that is 224 million people, and 90 million of them live in conditions of absolute poverty. Over half of the poor and absolutely poor are children and adolescents.

As indicated by the UN Fund for Children: "Children are more severely affected by poverty. No other age group is as vulnerable since the physical and psychological damage they sustain affects them for life."

According to information from the Pan American Health Organization, acute respiratory infections, diarrhea and nutritional deficiency persist as the three main causes of death for children under five years of age.

The average mortality rate for children under five years of age in Latin America and the Caribbean region in 1998 was 39 per 1,000 live births: the number of dead children was close to half a million.

Acute respiratory infections, such as influenza and pneumonia, are the cause of one third of all deaths among children under five in the region. Close to 60 percent of pediatric consultations are related and most of the resultant deaths could be prevented by a timely diagnosis and adequate treatment.

Between 20 and 50 percent of the urban population in the region live in dreadful conditions of massive overcrowding, extreme poverty, violence and marginalization. They do not have access to basic primary health care or sewage services. In the rural areas over 60 percent do not have these services and 50 percent lack drinking water. The absence of adequate sewage systems, drinking water supplies and medical care, raises the risk of death from diarrhea, cholera, typhoid fever and other transmissible diseases by over 40 percent.

Food and nutritional deficiencies impact on children's defense mechanisms, exponentially increasing their sensitivity to non-transmissible chronic diseases. ECLA has estimated that this year, approximately 36 percent of all children under two years of age are in a high risk situation from lack of food, which is worse still in the rural areas where about 46 percent are in jeopardy due to generally precarious sanitation conditions and greater difficulties in gaining access to public health care.

The poor segments of the population are affected by illnesses associated to deprivation. In the case of vitamin A deficiency, which is considered one of the main causes of blindness, millions of children under five years of age in the region are affected.

The direct cost of vaccines for immunizing a child under one year of age against six preventable childhood diseases such as diphtheria, measles, whooping cough, poliomyelitis, tuberculosis and tetanus is lower than 80 cents. Nevertheless, the World Health Organization has reported that all over the Americas, including in the United States and Canada, immunization coverage of children under one year against these diseases ranges from 85 to 90 percent. It is estimated that over 15 million children in the hemisphere, under five years of age, are not protected from those six diseases.

The average maternal death rate for Latin America and the Caribbean region amounts to 200 per 100,000 births while in developed nations the figure is about 15. In our region, no less than 50,000 children are motherless due to this cause alone. Moreover, for every dead mother, hundreds of others who survive suffer from chronic problems resulting from undernourishment and inadequate care during pregnancy and delivery. In this way, millions of mothers suffer some kind of chronic health problem related to the absence of effective medical care during pregnancy and delivery.

Two basic indicators, infant and maternal mortality rates, show that every year 6.5 more children and 12.6 more mothers die in Latin America and the Caribbean region than in the developed nations per 1,000 live births. In addition, of the 12 million children born very year, almost two million are born to adolescent mothers.

HIV/AIDS keeps growing at a dangerous pace in the region and, according to data from UNAIDS, 1.7 million people are already infected. UNICEF has indicated that 65,000 new children are infected every year, 90 percent of them by their own mothers. Consequently, the number of orphans due to HIV/AIDS is already 195,000. In Latin America and the Caribbean region over 78,000 people have died of AIDS.

As for education, it is estimated that 20 percent of children join the educational system late, and that average schooling is approximately four grades. Pre-school education coverage in the region reaches an average of 15 percent.

Likewise, child labor expands like a real plague. Close to 20 million children under 15 years of age are working and over half of them are girls, most performing tasks that are not recognized or reported in the official statistics.

According to the Pan American Health Organization, violence has become one of the main causes of death among children five to 15 years old. Although exact figures on child abuse are not available, several studies conducted by UNICEF indicate that no less than six million children and adolescents are victims of severe aggression and 80,000 of them die every year due to domestic violence.

A study conducted in 1996 by the World Conference on Sexual Exploitation revealed that in the previous year, 47 percent of girls sexually exploited in seven countries in the region had been victims of rape and violence at home. Almost half of these girls had been initiated into commercial sexual practices between the ages of nine and 13, and from 50 to 80 percent of them were on drugs. Hundreds of thousands of boys and girls work and live on the streets and in some capitals 46 percent of women involved in prostitution are under 16 years old. I will avoid here the political and economic causes of this tragedy, since they are very familiar to you.

Finally, I would add — as is my duty — that if the infant mortality rate in the Latin American and Caribbean region were similar to the 6.4 per 1,000 live births in the first year of life and the 8.3 for children under five reached by Cuba, almost 400,000 children would have survived every year; 99.2 percent would have pre-school education coverage; 99.9 percent would be enrolled in school by the age of six and 99.7 percent would remain in school up to the sixth grade. Also, 98.9 percent of the total first grade enrollment would have passed the sixth grade and 99.9 percent would have entered junior high school, while 99.5 percent of these graduates would go on to senior high school or technical school. Children in need of special education would have schools to attend. Actually, there would be no illiterate people and the average educational level of the adult population would be higher than the ninth grade. Lastly, there would not be one child under 16 years of age working for a living.

Our difficult experience has demonstrated that a lot can be done with very few resources.

Yesterday I had the privilege of speaking about infancy, so I was not planning to take the floor on this subject, but this morning's important debate has obliged me to say a few words. I emphasize "a few" so that no one is scared!

Neoliberal globalization is leading the world to disaster. I am not speaking from the point of view of any kind of philosophy or dogma. When we speak here we forget many things. We forget that present here today are European nations and Latin American nations. We forget that only very exceptionally do Latin American countries reach certain levels of economic, industrial and social development very much above the rest of Latin America.

Chile, for example, indicated that it has reduced the number of poor people from five to three million. This achievement warrants our recognition and congratulations. The most serious studies show, however, that in Latin America as a whole the number of poor people grows every day and every year, and that about 50 percent of children live in poverty or absolute poverty.

We forget that, for example, the public debt of Latin America and the Caribbean, which in 1992 was $478 billion, is $750 billion today. We forget that such a huge growth in debt followed the repayment of $913 billion in that period. We forget that the IMF, well known to all, and its masters are out there. We forget that private foreign investment at the end of the last decade amounted to $115 billion, and grew to $865 billion in 1999. We forget that 71 percent of this sum was invested in the rich countries themselves and only 29 percent was invested in so-called developing countries. Again, of that 29 percent, 45 percent was invested in China, 40 percent in Latin America and 15 percent in Africa and Asia. Of the total private foreign investment, approximately 85 percent was not used in the creation of new industrial facilities and services, that is, in the creation of new jobs and wealth, but rather in the acquisition of existing businesses and services. A new phenomenon.

The needs of the vast majority of our nations have not been truly met. Even in countries such as Cuba, where distribution inequalities have been reduced to a minimum, there are still differences and when these are abysmal, and poverty produces marginality, the result is misery.

Marginality, the result of huge income differences, has devastating effects on education. There is not the slightest equality between the prospects of a poor child and one whose basic needs are covered; this inequality affects practically half the children in the Latin American and Caribbean region. This very real tragedy calls for an answer. It is clear that, even in these conditions, there is room to act for the children in Latin America. This should be done, and some countries have shown here that they are making extraordinary efforts to that end. In Cuba, where despite the blockade and the poverty, advances have been made such as I described yesterday, we are not content because we understand that there is still much to be done. It can be done, and we will do it with the support of the extraordinary audiovisual and technical aids available today.

I might add that in our country we have developed a system to teach reading and writing over the radio. This system is being tested in the Republic of Haiti with 300 people and the results have been spectacular. It is currently being extended to 3,000 people and they are working on its extension to the entire country. We developed it in Creole, the language of the Haitians. The results are truly hopeful. This being the case, there are great possibilities to reduce the number of illiterates with a minimum of resources — really, a minimum. One central station simply broadcasts that knowledge.

I am not talking about television, which would make it easier. In Cuba, we are gradually extending education on television so that practically the whole country is becoming a university. I am not talking about things to do but about things that are already being done, with spectacular results, based on humankind's immense thirst for knowledge.

Among other things, we are conducting a profound study on poverty, marginalization and education. Some very interesting words have been spoken here with regards to the family situations of young people. We want to get to the source of crime, the roots of crime.

A whole new world opens before our eyes, not only in this field, but in many others. Although we are not rich, the availability of abundant human capital resulting from our educational achievements allows us today to conceive of dreams that in the past would have seemed unattainable and utopian. Still, we are embarrassed by the little we have so far achieved.

Let us work with current realities and avoid walking on clouds of illusion and deceit. We should look into the unjust political and economic order imposed on the world, to find the real and fundamental causes of our lack of much needed resources, to give our children a more humane destiny.

8

"It becomes impossible to ignore the idea that advances made by humankind in political development, social justice and peaceful coexistence lag far behind its extraordinary scientific and technological achievements."

On History and Humanity, Public Forum, Havana Province January 27, 2001

Humanity has entered one of the most complicated periods in its history. We have begun the new millennium amid the din of an intense and prolonged battle. The coming years will be decisive not only for Cuba, but for all the peoples who live on this planet.

During the century that has just come to an end, many years were lost in wars, in the parceling out of the world, in the plunder and exploitation — both collective and individual — of the immense majority of human beings. All this took place when we still had more than enough time to foresee and confront many of the gravest problems that now weigh so heavily on the world. The enormous advances in science and technology were already beginning.

At the beginning of the 20th century, there were still abundant expanses of virgin land, forests, water and mineral deposits for use in a rational and sustainable manner. The air and seas were not saturated with contaminants and chemical wastes, to the inconceivable extent that they are today. World politics and economics moved forward at such a blind and chaotic pace that concepts like the environment, biological diversity, the preservation of nature, desertification, holes in the ozone layer and climatic changes were barely mentioned or even known a few decades ago. Under a system of chaotic production, which eventually gave rise to the current state of imperial, hegemonic and unipolar control, enormous amounts of resources were squandered. Nature was significantly damaged, and absurd and unsustainable models of consumption were established, which constitute entirely unattainable dreams for the immense majority of those living on the planet today and those who will live on it tomorrow.

In the course of barely a century, a large part of the hydrocarbon reserves that nature took hundreds of millions of years to create, have been burned and released into the air and seas as gas and by-product wastes. The quest to seek profit at any cost, with no ethical or moral principles or foresight whatsoever, has left a devastating wake for current and future generations.

Reflecting on what is happening in the world, it becomes impossible to ignore the idea that advances made by humankind in political development, social justice and peaceful coexistence lag far behind its extraordinary scientific and technological achievements.

Meanwhile, the world population has grown to beyond six billion people, two thirds of whom live in unbearable backwardness and poverty. In 50 years, no fewer than three billion people more will share our already contaminated planet while many of those under 20 today will still be alive. Today, 1.8 billion people are children and adolescents under 16 years of age, like many of the youngsters gathered here today, blossoms bursting with hope and joy.

Can there be any more urgent task than to preserve the minimal living conditions necessary for all of these human beings — children, adolescents and adults, young and old? A worn out and obsolete world order will not be capable of saving humanity or creating the natural conditions necessary for dignified and decent life on the planet. Real equality of opportunity and genuine justice for all human beings of every nation, ethnic group, culture and religion cannot continue to be put off, in any corner of the world. This is not an ideological matter, it has become a matter of life and death for the human species.

It is obvious that nothing can be expected from those who wield the power and privileges of hegemonic rule. The neoliberal globalization they have imposed on the world is unsustainable. The first symptoms of crisis are already visible, and that crisis will be even more profound to the extent that the real economy is transformed into a speculative economy, encompassing most of the financial operations taking place in the world every day.

The conflicts between centers of economic power will increase, and the fight for markets will be more fierce. The usual objectives of any system of production have been turned upside down: the economy does not function and grow to create goods and services; goods and services are consumed to make the economy function and grow.

Nevertheless, there is not the slightest indication that those who control the bulk of the world's power and resources are capable of understanding this reality, and even if they did understand it, they do not have the will to change it. Today, the transnationals are institutions with more capacity, wealth and power than all of the world's governments put together. The crisis will further accelerate as they continue to merge and increasingly dominate the world's finances, production and economy, moved by the blind and uncontrollable laws of the system that gave rise to them.

The most likely course of events is that in a relatively short time, a profound crisis will finally erupt, leading to the ruin of the majority of the world's nations. Poverty and hunger will expand, and possibilities for development will be further reduced for the poor countries, where the immense majority of the world's population live. The experiences that humanity has lived through so far teach us that neither cold analysis, rational thinking, foresight nor basic common sense can produce solutions. It is unfortunate, but history has proven that major solutions only come from major crises.

A different world order, with greater justice and solidarity, capable of sustaining the natural environment and safeguarding life on the planet, is the only possible alternative. For this to come about, our species' instinct for self-preservation must make itself felt with greater force than ever.

Our small country is striving to make its modest contribution to the future we dream of. For reasons of geographical location and very particular historical circumstances, the revolution for liberation initiated in Cuba on October 10, 1868 now occupies a place of honor in the political battle that the peoples of the world have been forced to wage. They must fight for their existence and identity as nations, for their right to sustainable economic and social development, and for a fair, rational and solidarity-based world order.

As it celebrates the 42nd anniversary of its triumph, and victoriously enters the new millennium, the Cuban Revolution is now politically stronger than ever, and our people have achieved the highest degree of unity and revolutionary awareness in their history.

A new administration has just assumed power in the United States, in a rather irregular fashion. Everything known about the backgrounds and thinking of the main figures in this administration — through many of their public statements made before and after the highly unusual electoral process in which the Cuban American terrorist mafia played a decisive role in the questionable victory of the current president — has created an atmosphere of doubt, distrust and fear.

Cuba could become a target of the frustration, resentment and hatred of the most extreme and reactionary sectors [in the United States], currently in a state of euphoria over the rise to power of a new ruling team with whom they share close ties. Nevertheless, our country and our courageous people, who have confronted extreme dangers for 42 years, look toward the future with greater calm, serenity and confidence than ever. Nothing troubles our sleep.

Although we do not expect any improvements from this new administration, we will not make hasty judgments in advance, or cast the first stone. Instead, we will preserve the same high moral ground in our political conduct and methods as always. We will carefully observe every step they take and every word they say. Absolutely nothing will catch us off guard, unaware or unprepared, in economic, political or any other terms.

The Cuba that is entering the new millennium is not the inexperienced, unarmed and practically illiterate Cuba of 1959. There is not a single illiterate in Cuba today, and there are now two university graduates for every sixth-grade graduate back then. Millions of men and women have learned to use weapons; hundreds of thousands have carried out various internationalist missions; tens of thousands of experienced cadres have been trained in the battle. Our people have high levels of education and general and political knowledge — the country is like one big school. We have learned to withstand and overcome the most inconceivable circumstances. No other nation is more educated or less dependent on trade and economic relations with the country that has risen up as the wealthiest and most crucial power for the rest of the world. No other nation is freer to declare its truths and defend the rights of the world's poor and exploited peoples in every international forum.

Cuba will not hesitate to continue the battle of ideas it has been waging for 14 months, demanding respect for its rights and an end to the murderous and genocidal laws implemented against it, and to fulfill the sacred oath that its people have sworn to their homeland.

9

"This is how they treat their own people, these governments that try to deceive the world by calling themselves defenders of human rights."

Message to Protesters at the Quebec "Free Trade Area of the Americas" Summit
April 17, 2001

We have just seen on television images of the brutal way in which the Canadian authorities have suppressed the peaceful demonstrations in Quebec, protesting against the crime that is to be perpetrated against the political and economic rights of the people of Latin America and the Caribbean. This is disgraceful!

I wish to express, in the name of the people of Cuba, our fellow feeling and admiration for the valiant behavior of those who are struggling there for this just cause.

This is how they treat their own people, these governments that try to deceive the world by calling themselves defenders of human rights. This is how they try to clear their consciences of the millions of children, women, adults and old people around the world who die every year of sickness and hunger when they could have been saved. They will not be able to go on sustaining this unjust order they have imposed on humanity.

We convey our utmost solidarity. Cuba is with you, embraces you and sends you our greetings.

10

"If the present is tragic, the future looks dismal."

Inter-Parliamentary Union, Havana
April 5, 2001

When I spoke at the 68th Inter-Parliamentary Conference in 1981, after mentioning a number of figures to illustrate the growing gap separating the developed, wealthy world from the countries that were formerly its colonies, I made a statement that might have seemed excessive: "If the present is tragic, the future looks dismal."

Let nobody try to fool or confuse us with new terminology spawned by the specialists' hypocritical propaganda of deception and lies. They work in the service of those who have subjected humanity to an increasingly unequal and unfair economic and political order, one that is completely devoid of solidarity or democracy or respect for even the minimum rights owed to human beings.

I was not exaggerating when I made that statement. The Third

World's foreign debt, which totaled some $500 billion in 1981, had reached $2.1 trillion in the year 2000. The share corresponding to Latin America was $255,188 billion in 1981; by 2000, it was $750,855 billion.

The servicing of the Third World debt, which amounted to $44.2 billion in 1981, had reached $347.4 billion in 2000.

The per capita gross national product (GDP) in the developed countries was $8,070 in 1978. Twenty years later, in 1998, per capita GDP in those countries had grown to $25,870. In the meantime, the per capita GDP in the countries with the lowest incomes, which was $200 in 1978, had risen to only $530 by the year 1998. The abysmal gap had grown even wider.

The number of undernourished people, almost all of whom live in Third World countries, rose from 570 million in 1981 to 800 million in 2000. The number of unemployed grew from 1.103 billion in 1981 to 1.6 billion in 2000.

Today, the wealthiest 20 percent of the world's population account for 86 percent of all spending on private consumption, while the poorest 20 percent account for only 1.3 percent. In the wealthy countries, per capita electricity consumption is 10 times higher than in all the poor countries combined.

According to UN figures, in 1960 the income of 20 percent of the world population living in the wealthiest nations was 30 times that of the poorest nations; by 1997 it was 74 times greater.

Studies carried out by the Food and Agricultural Organization between 1987 and 1998 reveal that two out of every five children in the underdeveloped world suffer from growth retardation, while one out of every three is underweight for his or her age.

There are 1.3 billion poor people in the Third World; that is, one out of every three lives in poverty. The World Bank, in its latest report on poverty, predicts that the number of people living in absolute poverty could reach 1.5 billion as the new millennium begins.

The wealthiest 25 percent of the world's population consumes 45 percent of all meat and fish; the poorest 25 percent consumes only five percent. In sub-Saharan Africa, the infant mortality rate is 107 per 1,000 live births during the first year of life, and 173 per 1,000 live births before the age of five. In South Asia, the rates are 76 and 114, respectively. In the case of Latin America, according to UNICEF, infant mortality before the age of five is 39 per 1,000 live births.

More than 800 million adults remain illiterate. More than 130 million school-age children are growing up without access to basic education. The truth, which cannot be hidden, is that there are currently over 800 million people suffering chronic hunger while lacking access to health care services, which is why it is estimated that 507 million people living in the Third World today will not live past 40 years of age. South of the Sahara, almost 30 percent of the population will die before they are 40.

In 1981, climate change was seldom mentioned, and very few people had ever even heard of AIDS. Today these are two harrowing threats that have been added to the calamities already mentioned.

In 1981, the world population had surpassed four billion; 75 percent of them living in Third World countries. Today, in 2001, there are already more than 6.1 billion of us on the planet. In just 20 years, the world population has grown by 1.7 billion, more than it had grown from the emergence of the human species until the beginning of the 20th century.

In short, the world income share of the countries that now constitute the Third World has shrunk so much that a century and a half ago it was 56 percent, while today it is only 15 percent. This is truly a peculiar way of expressing the real meaning of capitalism and imperialism for the Third World and the immense majority of humanity: crises, chaos, economic anarchy and selfish and inhuman value systems.

After four centuries of Spanish colonial domination and 57 years as a U.S. colony, our country, for the first time in history, achieved its double freedom, for we freed ourselves from both the [Batista] dictatorship and the empire [the United States]. From that moment on, our poor nation has been subjected to a brutal economic blockade.

Many believed that we were only a simple satellite of a great power. The fall of the revolution was expected within a matter of weeks, or months at the most. But the satellite proved that it had its own light, its own extraordinary power, a small sun of true freedom, sovereignty, patriotism, social justice, equality of opportunities, solidarity within and beyond its borders, and unshakable ethical and human principles.

Has this power, this enormous prestige, this strength and unity of the people, achieved through the revolution, served to satisfy personal vanity, or greed for power or material goods? No, it has served to withstand the assault launched by the empire at one of the most dangerous and difficult moments in the history of our country.

Let no one even try to give us lessons on history or politics, treating Cuba's leaders like preschool children. It is actually possible that Cuban pre-school children know more about these matters than some well-known politicians.

Under horrendous circumstances, a social project has been carried out [in Cuba] that is overwhelming, irrefutable, insurmountable. Illiteracy was eradicated in just one year, in a country where almost a third of the population between the ages of 15 and 60 could not read and write. At the same time, thousands of classrooms were created in isolated places and almost inaccessible regions. Medical services were established in the countryside and the cities, despite the fact that the United States had taken away half of the 6,000 doctors in the country at the time and over half of the medical school professors, with visas and promises of a better material life. Teachers and professors were trained for elementary school, and junior and senior high-school. Thousands of schools were built, and polytechnic institutes, and training centers for teachers and professors of music, dance, art, physical education and sports. Dozens of higher education institutions were established throughout the country, where previously there had been only three. These included 21 medical schools — which now total 22, with the creation of the Latin American School of Medical Sciences — and 15 university level teacher-training schools.

In less than 40 years, Cuba became the first country in Latin America and the Third World to reduce infant mortality to 6.4 per 1,000 live births in the first year of life, and to achieve a life expectancy of 75, in the midst of the "special period." Cuba has brought free medical care to all its citizens; raised the average educational level to ninth grade; graduated over 700,000 university-trained professionals; developed a powerful artistic and cultural movement; and is placed among the top 10 countries in the Olympics, winning more gold medals per capita than any other. In regional competitions and international events, Cuba has garnered thousands of medals, occupying second place in this hemisphere, behind the United States. Its children achieve top scores in mathematics and science competitions.

According to UNESCO research, our primary school students

have almost twice as much knowledge as the average student in the rest of Latin America. Today our country is first among all countries in the world, both developed and underdeveloped, in terms of the number of professors and teachers, doctors, and high-level physical education and sports instructors. These are three decisive areas for the well-being and social and economic development of any nation.

In all, we have 250,000 educators, 67,500 medical doctors, and 34,000 physical education and sports professors and technicians.

Presently, we are sharing this immense human capital with our sister nations of the Third World, without charging a cent. Cubans working overseas boast not only extensive technical and scientific capacity, but also the most important traits of all: extraordinary human solidarity and an unsurpassed spirit of sacrifice.

Hundreds of thousands of our compatriots have discharged internationalist missions in many Third World countries, particularly in Africa, as technical personnel and especially as combatants against colonialism and the racist, fascist apartheid system.

You may be wondering why I am elaborating so much on these facts.

Firstly: Because I wonder if this is why some try to condemn us every year [at the Human Rights Commission] in Geneva.

Secondly: Because I wonder if this is why we have been subjected to harassment, economic warfare and a blockade for 42 years now.

Thirdly: Because I wonder if this is why some want to destroy the Cuban Revolution.

I should add something else. In 42 years of revolution, not once has there been a case of tear gas used against the people, or the spectacle of police with riot gear, horses or armored cars suppressing the people, things that are seen very frequently in Europe and the United States. There have never been death squads in our country, or any missing people, or a single political assassination, or a single victim of torture, despite what is said by a frustrated and unscrupulous empire that would like to wipe the image and example of Cuba off the face of Earth.

You may travel around the country, ask the people, look for a single piece of evidence, try to find a single case where the Revolutionary Government has ordered or tolerated such an action, and if you find them, then I will never speak in public again.

Only a fool would believe that the Cuban people could be

governed by force or in any way other than through consensus that arises from the elevated political consciousness of our people, the work achieved, and the enviable relationship between the masses and their leadership. In the elections for the assemblies of People's Power, over 95 percent of the country's eligible voters willingly and enthusiastically cast their ballots.

The ethics and politics of imperialism are quite a different matter.

When Cuban troops were fighting in Angola, in 1988, when the decisive battle against the South African troops was being waged in Cuito Cuanavale, and 40,000 Cuban soldiers and 30,000 Angolans were marching on the Namibian border in southwest Angola, the racist South Africans had seven nuclear warheads similar to the bombs dropped on Hiroshima and Nagasaki. NATO knew it, the United States knew it, but no one said a word about it, in the hope that the bombs would be used against the Cuban-Angolan forces.

During the 15 long years we were in southern Africa, mounting the guard against the forces of apartheid or actively fighting them, the major capitalist countries had large investments in South Africa and their trade with this racist regime amounted to billions of U.S. dollars every year. The U.S. investments in South Africa at that time totaled $3 billion and their annual trade $6 billion, while an additional $3 billion in bank credits had been granted to that country.

It is common knowledge that the United States was a military ally of South Africa — could this possibly be forgotten? — and that through South Africa it supplied UNITA [Angolan opposition] with copious amounts of weapons, including portable anti-aircraft missiles and millions of antipersonnel mines, which it planted throughout Angolan territory. UNITA wiped out entire villages and killed hundreds of thousands of civilians, including women and children. I am not exaggerating in the slightest.

Once Cuba's internationalist mission had been concluded with honor, and an agreement reached leading to the implementation of UN resolution 435, and to Namibian independence, we rigorously complied with the commitments made by the parties involved and withdrew our forces. When our forces left Africa, they took nothing with them but the remains of their comrades who had fallen in combat. We did not own a single square meter of land there — as I said a few days ago — or a single screw in a factory. No Western country had shed a single drop of blood there. Only one country had done this, a small and faraway country, located 10,000 kilometers from Africa: Cuba.

Now, added to everything I said at the beginning of this speech about the dramatic economic and social situation currently facing the peoples of the Third World, the new U.S. administration is taking arrogant steps in the international sphere. These could create serious complications, just when the international economy, and above all the U.S. economy, faces the serious threat of stagnation, recession and crisis. The effects of this are beginning to be felt around the world, with drops in the volume of exports, falling prices for basic commodities, a fall in stock prices, and massive layoffs and down-sizing everywhere.

The most serious events have taken place over the course of just a few weeks.

First: The decision to create a nuclear missile shield, which would unilaterally break the commitments entered into under the Anti-Ballistic Missile Treaty, and inexorably lead to an arms race.

Second: The decision to veto the draft resolution proposing the establishment of an observer force for the protection of the Palestinian people, which was backed by China, Russia and seven other members of the Security Council, with four abstentions, including two other permanent members.

Since May 1990, the United States has exercised its right to veto on five occasions, four of them in relation to the Palestinian-Israeli conflict. The last time the United States applied its veto was on March 21, 1997, in support of Israeli interests and to the detriment of the Palestinians, against a resolution demanding that Israel stop the building of a settlement in East Jerusalem.

Since 1972, the United States has used its veto on 23 occasions against resolutions aimed at solving the Palestinian issue.

The complicated situation in the Middle East has been further aggravated by this latest U.S. veto, when an extreme right-wing government has just taken power in Israel.

Third: The unilateral decision to break the commitments made at the third session of the Conference of the Parties to the United Nations Framework Convention on Climate Change, held in Kyoto in late 1997, where 34 industrialized countries agreed to reduce emissions of greenhouse gases by 5.2 percent by the year 2012 — a goal that is crucial for humanity. The United States had committed itself to reducing those emissions by seven percent. Its back down was a real blow to world public opinion, especially to the European countries which had made the greatest contributions to the reduction of greenhouse gas emissions.

Fourth: Official statements that are insulting and humiliating for Russia and China, using typical Cold War language, a reflection of the mentality clearly surfacing in many of the members of the team surrounding and advising the current president of the United States.

Fifth: Tangible contempt, which cannot be disguised, towards Latin America, in proposing [Negroponte] as the new administration's assistant Under-Secretary of State for Latin American affairs, a sinister individual with a fascist mentality. The man is notorious for his participation, alongside Oliver North, as a special adviser to the Secretary of State during the Reagan Administration. He was involved in the scandal of the sale of weapons to raise funds for the dirty war against the Sandinista Government in Nicaragua. These arms sales were in fact prohibited at the time by agreements adopted by the U.S. Congress itself. The man has published documents and statements that he himself had signed in the names of Nicaraguan counterrevolutionary leaders, some of whom could neither read nor write. He has broken the law, and shown a total lack of ethics. A number of U.S. press agencies have harshly criticized this decision, and many Latin American leaders are not at all happy about it.

In any event, these steps clearly reflect the traits and personality of the new occupant of the presidential throne in the United States of America.

11

"Pinochet did not act alone. The president of the United States, his government and the highest state authorities, made the decision to overthrow Allende the day he was elected."

The Trial of General Augusto Pinochet
for War Crimes
April 28, 2001

The Notimex press agency reported that Judge Garzón [Spanish judge in General Pinochet's trial], when asked by a journalist from the Santo Domingo daily Listín Diario *whether he would dare send Fidel Castro to jail, responded that no legal action for crimes of any kind can be brought against acting heads of state. He added that these matters are governed by the same rules as the treaties of 1969 and the rule of nonresponsibility of heads of state. Only an international court could take such an action.*

Garzón admitted that he had received case files against the Cuban leader, but had not studied them in depth, given the fact that no legal action could be taken because of the restrictions established by international rules.

Regarding the case files sent to Judge Garzón, I am well aware that the Cuban American terrorist mafia was behind this maneuver, and that they had placed a great deal of hope in him.

I do not feel and never have felt the slightest bit worried about Mr. Garzón. Quite simply, I am not under his jurisdiction, or that of Spanish law. There is no international principle that grants him the power to pass judgment on a citizen of another country who does not live in Spain and has committed no wrongdoing whatsoever there. Spanish national law has no extraterritorial jurisdiction, just as the Helms-Burton Act and the national law of the United States do not. Such extraterritorial jurisdiction would only serve as a dangerous weapon in the hands of the most powerful states, against small countries that rebel against their interests. The leaders of any revolutionary movement who are not to the liking of imperialism — no matter how ethical their conduct or how just their cause — could be prosecuted at its whim, in accordance with its own national laws and the decisions of its judges, who are so often venal and corrupt.

The universal hatred inspired by the dreadful crimes committed by Pinochet and the Argentine military regime, who tortured and vanished tens of thousands of people, should not serve as justification for granting the United States and its NATO allies extraterritorial jurisdiction for their laws and judges.

During the Ibero-American Summit in Oporto, in the early morning hours on the day I met with King Juan Carlos of Spain, someone brought me the news that Pinochet had been arrested in Britain. I thought: How strange, since Pinochet was the one who helped the English most during the war in the Falkland Islands!

The next day I answered questions posed by a number of journalists on Pinochet's arrest in Britain and possible trial in Spain, and I said: "From a moral standpoint, his arrest and punishment are acts of justice.

"From a legal standpoint, this action is questionable.

"From a political standpoint, I think it is going to create a complicated situation in Chile, given the way in which the political process has developed there." I further added: "Pinochet did not act alone. The president of the United States, his government and the highest state authorities, made the decision to overthrow Allende the day he was elected. They allocated abundant funds for this purpose, and gave instructions to use any means possible, first, to prevent him from taking power, and second, to attempt to overthrow him throughout his term in office." I was a firm supporter of the view that Pinochet should be tried and sentenced in Chile.

I understand the feelings of those who have seen so many crimes committed with absolute impunity against the people. It had become a pattern in Latin American political history. The Cuban people suffered more than once. But with the triumph of the revolution, just as the people had been promised, the war criminals were tried and sentenced, excepting those who after torturing and murdering tens of thousands of Cubans received sanctuary in the United States. The ill-gotten riches of the embezzlers were confiscated. It was the first time in the history of Latin America that justice was so fully and methodically applied.

Everyone knows that the U.S. Government not only promoted the coup d'état in Chile, but also promoted and backed the military regimes in Argentina and Uruguay; the counterrevolution in Guatemala; the dirty war in Nicaragua and the bloody repression in El Salvador. The United States supplied all of them with weapons and economic aid, and trained thousands of torturers — in U.S. territory — in the most refined techniques for obtaining information and sowing terror. Not even Hitler's Gestapo reached such extremes of cruelty. These regimes vanished more than 150,000 people and took the lives of hundreds of thousands more. This has been proven and confessed in declassified official documents. One would be justified in asking why not one of the U.S. officials guilty of such political crimes was included in Pinochet's trial.

A world legal order should be established against genocide and war crimes, with rigorous and precise rules, along with a fully independent body of justice, under the supervision of the United Nations General Assembly. It should never be established under the Security Council, as long as veto power remains in effect, granting exceptional privileges to just five countries, including the superpower, which has used the veto power more often than the rest of the Council's permanent members combined.

Cuba has been the target of an economic war that has lasted more than 42 years, as well as serious crimes and acts of genocide like the blockade on food and medicine. Such acts are referred to and defined as genocidal, and are subject to punishment, even in times of war, as stated in the 1948 and 1949 treaties signed by both the United States and Cuba. Furthermore, these treaties grant the courts of the victimized countries the right to try the guilty parties, in the absence of an international tribunal empowered to do so.

The Pinochet case should serve as an example, but it should not lead the underdeveloped and militarily weak nations, which constitute the vast majority of the world's states, to run the suicidal risk of granting the superpower and its NATO allies the privilege of being the judges of all other countries. Rather, it should lead to the demand that the United Nations adopt the relevant measures to ensure justice and protection for all of the peoples of the world against war crimes and acts of genocide. Cuba would be the first to support this initiative.

Having said so, I thank Judge Garzón for his judicious response to the journalist from *Listín Diario*, even though he did not bother to study in depth the case files put forward by the Miami anti-Castro mafia.

I will excuse Mr. Garzón because he does not know the Cuban people, and he has certainly studied very little of the history of their struggles against hundreds of thousands of brave Spanish soldiers. Despite the enormous difference in the number of men and weapons, the Cuban patriots never fled from danger.

Even though, after an opportunistic intervention, Cuba was ceded by the colonial power to the United States, and the nascent empire imposed on us a constitutional amendment giving it the right to intervene, Cubans today are a free people, defending their independence against the aggression, hostility and hatred of the now gigantic power that is our neighbor.

No mortal should think themselves more fearsome than the gods.

I have always lived and will continue to live in peace, for the rest of my life, because I know how to defend with dignity the rights of my people and the honor of small, poor or weak nations, and I have always been inspired by a profound sense of justice. I am a revolutionary and I will die a revolutionary. If a judge or authority from Spain or any other NATO ally ever attempted to have me arrested, using arbitrary extraterritorial powers and violating sacred rights, they should know beforehand that there will be a fight, no matter where they try to do it, for I do believe in the extraterritoriality of the honor and dignity of all people.

12

"How very wonderful that two or three Disneylands will surely be built in Central and South America!"

On Globalization and Latin America, Havana
May 1, 2001

After 42 years of resistance to a cruel and genocidal blockade, Cuba has entered the new millennium with renewed energy and greater strength. In 1959, a new era of struggle began. Our people, freed from neocolonial status, saturated with McCarthyist propaganda and lies, poorly educated and almost illiterate politically, made a colossal leap in history: they eradicated illiteracy and graduated hundreds of thousands of professionals with a far greater level of political consciousness than their historical adversary.

Our people have now achieved the highest degree of unity ever, with a vast political experience and moral, patriotic and internationalist strength. These are the people who resolutely endured the Bay of Pigs invasion, the Missile Crisis, the dirty war, an ever more rigorous economic blockade, the demise of the Soviet Union and the socialist bloc, and predictions of an inevitable collapse.

Today, we face an enemy that is powerful in every way, except in ethics and ideas, which has no response for the grave political, economic and social problems weighing down the world. Internationally, there has never been such confusion, discontent and insecurity. On the brink of a profound political and economic crisis, imperialism cannot escape from its own shadow. It is condemned to plunder the rest of the world to an ever greater extent, fomenting universal discontent and rebellion, even among its allies.

Throughout almost two centuries, the indigenous population and other peoples of Latin America and the Caribbean have been victims of the US policy of expansion to the west and south of the original 13 colonies that declared their independence from British rule in 1776. In their advance toward the west they practically exterminated the indigenous peoples. Later, in 1835, they promoted the independence of Texas, where U.S. settlers were already living in large numbers. In 1847, they invaded Mexico, unleashing a brutal war. As a result, in February 1848, they took possession of 55 percent of Mexico's territory. And so they continued, exterminating the native peoples or displacing them from the lands they had lived on for centuries; annexing territories of former European colonies like they had done with Texas, or conquering it like the territory stolen from Mexico. The United States, nurtured by large migrations from Europe in the second half of the 19th century, had become a powerful and prosperous nation. The states from Patagonia to the Canadian border, which had rid themselves of Spanish colonial domination after the independence struggles begun by Venezuela in 1810, remained divided and isolated.

On June 20, 1898, the United States launched a military intervention in Cuba just when, after lengthy struggle, our country was on the verge of achieving independence from an exhausted and bankrupt Spain. Our country remained occupied by the U.S. forces for almost four years.

In 1902, the troops of the United States of America left the island, but only after establishing a neocolony whose natural resources, lands and services were retained under its control, with the additional support of an amendment imposed on our constitution, granting the United States the legal right to militarily intervene in our country.

The party created by Martí had been dismantled; the Liberation Army, which had fought for 30 years, was disarmed only to be replaced with an army organized and trained by the United States, in the image of its own. The arbitrary and unfair right to intervene was used under any pretext on more than one occasion.

Puerto Rico, Cuba's twin sister in the liberation struggle, both countries "the two wings of a bird," was turned into a U.S. colony, and still retains this unfortunate status today. Haiti, the Dominican Republic, Guatemala, Nicaragua, other Central American nations and even Mexico, have been the victims of direct or indirect military interventions by the United States on repeated occasions. The isthmus of Panama was occupied in order to complete construction of and guarantee access to the strategic canal that the United States controlled for almost a century. The pervasive U.S. presence in the rest of the South American nations was achieved through large investments, coups, military regimes and growing political, ideological and cultural interference. After World War II, the United States ran all of these countries to its liking.

The first major curb on U.S. expansionism and political and economic control of Latin America came about in Cuba, with the triumph of the revolution on January 1, 1959. This ushered in a new stage in the history of the hemisphere.

Everything that has been done in this hemisphere by successive U.S. administrations, right up until now, has been strongly influenced by their obsession and fear over the troubling presence of the Cuban Revolution — from the days of the Bay of Pigs invasion and the Alliance for Progress, to Bush's statements from the bunker in Quebec [during the 2001 anti-corporate protests], where he invoked the name of José Martí, misquoting Martí's thoughts about freedom. Actually, although the triumph of the revolution troubled them, its remarkable resistance for over four decades sometimes creates the impression of driving them insane.

With a hatefulness that will go down in history, all of the governments of Latin America, with the exception of Mexico, joined more or less willingly in the isolation and blockade of Cuba. The OAS [Organization of American States] was so severely damaged that it has never recovered. Today, when a massive annexation of Latin American countries to the United States is being planned, no one can explain the continued existence and spending of money on that morally bankrupt institution. What the OAS did back then, as an instrument of the United States, is what the United States wants the FTAA [Free Trade Area of the Americas] to do today. Not to isolate Cuba, but rather to liquidate sovereignty, to prevent integration and to devour the resources and frustrate the destinies of a group of peoples who — leaving out the English-speaking — add up to more than 500 million people with a shared Latin-based language, culture and history.

If the OAS sold its soul to the devil back then, betraying Cuba so that the Latin American countries could receive, along with other favors, the several-million-ton Cuban sugar quota on the U.S. market, then what can be expected today of those bourgeois and oligarchic governments, who voted alongside the United States [at the Human Rights Commission] in Geneva? Out of opportunism or cowardice, they provided the extreme-right U.S. Government with the pretexts and justifications needed to maintain the genocidal blockade, and even a potential excuse for aggression against the people of Cuba, all served up on a silver platter.

Dragged along by the ill-fated annexationist current, it is only logical that the desperation created by enormous and unpayable debts and total economic dependence, will lead to the death of the FTAA. Talk of free trade is music to the ears of some Latin American politicians, as if they were still living in the middle of the last century, calling for the removal of U.S. tariff barriers and depending solely on the export of basic commodities. They do not realize that the world has changed, that many of those commodities, like fibers, rubber and other materials, have been replaced by synthetics; that foodstuffs like sugar have been replaced by high fructose corn syrup, with a higher sweetening power and fewer calories preferred by many people, or by artificial flavors like vanilla, strawberry and others that imitate tropical and semi-tropical fruits. Their mindsets are frozen on the demands of half a century ago. Neoliberal poisons and lies have blinded them, and large sectors of the population are stultified. They do not understand the basics of the problems they suffer, because nothing is explained to them, or information is hidden from them.

There is absolutely no doubt that the governments of two of the most important countries in Latin America, those of Bolívar's Venezuela and Brazil, the largest and most highly populated Latin

American nation, understand these realities, and are heading up the resistance.

For Cuba, it is clear that the so-called Free Trade Area of the Americas, under the terms, timetable, strategy, objectives and procedures imposed by the United States, would inexorably lead to Latin America's annexation to the United States. This kind of association is between an enormous industrial, technological and financial power and countries that suffer tearing poverty and underdevelopment. They further suffer financial dependence on institutions under the aegis of the United States, which controls, directs and makes the decisions in the IMF, the World Bank, the Inter-American Development Bank and others. Such an association imposes such inequality that it is tantamount to nothing less than the total absorption of the economies of the Latin American and Caribbean countries by that of the United States.

All of the banks, insurance companies, telecommunications, shipping services and airlines will be U.S.-owned. All business will pass into the hands of U.S. companies, from the big retail store chains to pizza outlets and McDonalds.

The chemical industry, and the automotive, machine and equipment industries, as well as other basic industries will all be U.S.-owned.

U.S. transnational companies will own the major research, biotechnology and genetic engineering centers and large pharmaceutical companies. The patents and technologies, almost without exception, will be U.S.-owned. The best Latin American scientists will work in U.S. laboratories.

The big hotel chains will be U.S.-owned.

The so-called entertainment industry will be an almost complete U.S. monopoly. As an almost exclusive supplier, Hollywood will produce movies and television serials for the movie theaters, television networks and videocassette markets of Latin America. Our countries, where consumption of these products is already around 80 percent, will see an even greater growth in their prevalence, as destructive to their values and national cultures as they are. How very wonderful that two or three Disneylands will surely be built in Central and South America! The Latin American nations will continue to serve basically as sources of raw materials, producers of primary commodities and enormous profits for big transnational capital. The U.S. agricultural sector already receives some $80 billion in subsidies and will continue receiving them in the future, although due to the use of large and sophisticated machinery and abundant fertilization its per capita and per hectare productivity is much higher. It will grow genetically modified grains, with much higher crop yields, heedless of the implications for human health.

Consequently, crops of corn, wheat, rice, soybean and other grains will practically disappear from many Latin American countries, which will be left with no food security.

When a major drought or other disasters affect agricultural production in entire regions of the world, large countries like China, with abundant hard currency reserves, or India, with fewer reserves but a certain amount of financial resources, could find themselves obliged to buy tens of millions of tons of grains. If this happened, and if their own grain production is wiped out by the FTAA, the prices of these products could reach unattainable levels for many Latin American countries. No matter how large their crop yields, the United States can only produce a small percentage of the food needed by a growing world population, which is now over 6.1 billion people. A decrease in food production in Latin America would affect not only the Latin American countries, but also the rest of the world.

Latin America will continue, under ever more intolerable conditions, to play the sad role of a supplier of raw materials and increasingly cheap labor. Wages in the United States are 15 or 20 times higher than what the big transnational companies pay in factories they have opened throughout the region. What's more, these factories employ fewer and fewer people as automation expands and productivity grows. The notion that large numbers of jobs will be created is an illusion. The agricultural sector, which tends to provide employment for a higher number of workers, will be affected by those elements mentioned earlier. As a result, unemployment will grow considerably. Germany and other European countries have unemployment rates of up to 10 percent, despite the enormously high number of industries and services there.

The Latin American nations will be compelled to become large free trade areas with low taxes or no taxes at all. These countries have already begun to compete with each other, seeking foreign investment at any cost. Perhaps they will be visited by larger numbers of U.S. tourists who will travel throughout the vast territory of Central and South America, staying in U.S.-owned hotels, traveling on U.S.-owned airlines and cruise ships, using U.S.-owned communications services, eating in U.S.-owned restaurants, and shopping in U.S.-owned stores, where they will buy goods produced by U.S.-owned companies with Latin American petroleum and raw materials. Latin America will export oil, copper, bauxite, meat (as long as it is free of foot and mouth disease), bananas and other fruit, if there are no tariff protection measures in place, and perhaps a few handicrafts.

What will be left? The worst paid and most grueling jobs in U.S.-owned companies, or employment as servants in the homes of U.S. executives and managers, highly qualified professionals, or what is left of the local bourgeoisie. Only a minority of the privileged bourgeoisie and the labor aristocracy will stand to gain anything. Large masses of workers will be laid off, as is the case today in Argentina, where the unemployment rate is between 15 and 20 percent, without any kind of unemployment benefits.

These are the fruits of neoliberalism, despite the tens of billions of dollars of foreign capital invested, the privatization and sale to foreign companies of almost all state companies, and the enormous debt contracted through the large loans received. The FTAA will mean more neoliberalism, less protection of national industry and interests, more unemployment, and more social problems.

It is absolutely certain that national currencies will be lost. None of them will survive, they will all be replaced by the U.S. dollar. Even without the FTAA, there is already a rising trend in numerous countries that are following in the steps of Ecuador's decision [to "dollarize" its economy]. The U.S. Federal Reserve will dictate the monetary policy of every one of these countries. The FTAA, which will only benefit big transnational capital, will not help U.S. workers either, as many will be laid off. This is why their representatives protested so strongly in Quebec, just as they fiercely protested against the WTO in Seattle.

If Cuba did not have an independent monetary policy, it would never have achieved the sevenfold appreciation in the value of the peso between 1994 and 1999, and it would never have been possible to endure the "special period."

Two decisive elements were at play: nonmembership in the IMF and an independent monetary policy. When everything I have said about the FTAA actually happens, it will no longer be possible to speak of independence, and annexation will begin to be a reality. This is absolutely not an overstatement.

The worst, the saddest, the most shameless and hypocritical thing of all, is that Latin American countries intend to take this step without consulting their peoples. This is all the democracy that can be expected from the imperial power and its lackeys.

I am firmly convinced that Latin America and the Caribbean can be devoured by the decadent empire. But they will never be digested, because the peoples will ensure that our continent's nations rise up from their ashes and integrate, as they must integrate and unite in search of a greater and more dignified destiny. It would, however, be much better if the hundreds of millions of Caribbean and Latin Americans were spared the difficult stage of the subsequent struggle for our liberation.

We must prevent annexation, and resolutely demand from this moment forward, that no government be allowed to sell out a nation behind its people's back! There must be no annexation without a plebiscite! We must build an awareness of the dangers that the FTAA will entail.

We must revive Bolívar's dignity and his dreams, and the dignity and dreams of San Martín, O'Higgins, Sucre, Morazán, Hidalgo, Morelos, Juárez and Martí.

Let nobody be fooled into thinking that the peoples will sit back, doing nothing, allowing themselves to be sold like slaves at an auction!

Today, we will stage the first protest. In a few minutes, we will set out with hundreds of thousands of Cubans on a Latin American protest march on the United States Interests Section [in Havana], shouting this slogan: Annexation no, plebiscite yes! Annexation no, plebiscite yes! Let it ring out loud and clear, and be heard all the way up in Washington!

Today, in the company of hundreds of leaders and representatives of the workers of Latin America, the Caribbean, the United States, Canada, Europe, Asia and Africa, we say: Latin American and Caribbean independence or death!

13

"Cuba speaks of reparations, and supports this idea as an unavoidable moral duty to the victims of racism, based on a major precedent — that is the indemnification being paid to the descendants of the Hebrew people, who in the very heart of Europe suffered the brutal and racist holocaust."

World Conference against Racism, Racial Discrimination, Xenophobia and Related Intolerance, Durban, South Africa
September 1, 2001

Racism, racial discrimination and xenophobia are not natural, instinctive reactions of human beings, but rather are social, cultural and political phenomena born directly of wars, military conquests, slavery and the individual or collective exploitation of the weakest by the most powerful throughout the history of human societies.

No one has the right to boycott this conference, which tries to bring some sort of relief to the overwhelming majority of humankind afflicted by unbearable suffering and enormous injustice. Neither has anyone the right to set preconditions for this conference or urge it to avoid discussion of historical responsibility, fair compensation or the way we decide to rate the dreadful genocide perpetrated, at this very moment, against our Palestinian brothers and sisters. This genocide is perpetrated by leaders of the extreme right [in Israel] who, in alliance with the hegemonic superpower, pretend to act on behalf of a people, which for almost 2,000 years was the victim of the fiercest persecution, discrimination and injustice that history has known.

Cuba speaks of reparations, and supports this idea as an unavoidable moral duty to the victims of racism, based on a major precedent — that is the indemnification being paid to the descendants of the Hebrew people, who in the very heart of Europe suffered the brutal and racist holocaust. We do not speak, however, with the intent to undertake an impossible search for the direct descendants of the victims of actions that have occurred throughout centuries. The irrefutable truth is that tens of millions of Africans were captured, sold like commodities and sent beyond the Atlantic to work in slavery, while 70 million indigenous people in that hemisphere perished as a result of the European conquest and colonization.

The inhuman exploitation imposed on the peoples of three continents, including Asia, marked forever the destiny and lives of over 4.5 billion people living in the Third World today. Those people suffer terrible poverty, unemployment, illiteracy and health rates as well as infant mortality, low life expectancy and other calamities — too many, in fact, to enumerate here — which are awesome and harrowing. They are the current victims of an atrocity which lasted centuries and they are the ones who clearly deserve compensation for the horrendous crimes perpetrated against their ancestors and peoples.

Such brutal exploitation did not end when many countries became independent, not even after the formal abolition of slavery. Right after U.S. independence — when the 13 colonies rid themselves of British domination at the end of the 18th century — the main ideologists of the American Union promoted ideas and strategies that were unquestionably expansionist in nature.

It was based on such ideas that the white settlers of European descent, in their march to the West, forcibly occupied the lands in which Native Americans had lived for thousands of years, exterminating millions of them in the process. They did not stop at the boundaries of former Spanish possessions and consequently Mexico, a Latin American country that had attained its independence in 1821, was stripped of millions of square kilometers of territory and invaluable natural resources. Meanwhile, within the increasingly powerful and expansionist nation of the United States, the obnoxious and inhumane system of slavery stayed in place for almost a century after the famous 1776 Declaration of Independence was issued — the same document that proclaimed all men were born free and equal.

After the purely formal slave emancipation, African Americans were subjected, for 100 more years, to the harshest racial discrimination. Many of the features and consequences of that discrimination still persist, even four decades after the heroic struggles and achievements of the 1960s and 1970s, for which Martin Luther King, Jr., Malcolm X and other outstanding fighters gave their lives. Based on a purely racist rationale, the longest and most severe legal sentences are passed against African Americans who, in a wealthy U.S. society, are bound to live in dire poverty and with the lowest living standards.

Likewise, what is left of the Native American peoples, who were the first inhabitants of large portions of the current territory of the United States, suffer even worse conditions of discrimination and neglect.

The statistics on the social and economic situation of Africa, show that entire countries and even whole regions of Sub-Saharan Africa risk extinction as the result of an extremely complex combination of economic backwardness, excruciating poverty and grave diseases, both old and new, that have become true plagues. The situation is no less dramatic in numerous Asian countries. On top of all this, exist huge and unpayable debts, disparate terms of trade, ruinous prices of basic commodities, the demographic explosion, neoliberal globalization and the climate changes that produce long droughts alternating with increasingly intensive rains and floods. Such a predicament is unsustainable.

The developed countries and their consumer societies, presently responsible for the accelerated and almost unstoppable destruction of the environment, have been the main beneficiaries of conquest and colonization, slavery, the ruthless exploitation and extermination of hundreds of millions of people born in the countries that today constitute the Third World. They have also reaped the benefits of the economic order imposed on humanity after two atrocious and devastating wars for a new division of the world and its markets, of the privileges granted to the United States and its allies in Bretton

Woods, and of the IMF and the international financial institutions exclusively created by them and for them.

That rich and squandering world is in possession of the technical and financial resources necessary to pay what is due to humankind. The hegemonic superpower should also pay back its special debt to African Americans, to Native Americans living in reservations, and to the tens of millions of Latin American and Caribbean immigrants as well as others from poor nations, be they mulatto, yellow or black, victims all of vicious discrimination and scorn.

It is high time to put an end to the dramatic situation of the indigenous communities in our hemisphere. Their own awakening and struggle, and the universal admission of the monstrosity of the crime committed against them make this imperative.

There are enough funds to save the world from tragedy.

May the arms race and the commerce in weapons that bring only devastation and death truly end.

Let a good part of the $1 trillion spent annually on commercial advertising that creates false illusions and inaccessible consumer habits, while releasing venom that destroys national cultures and identities, be used for development

May the modest 0.7 percent of the gross national product, promised as official development assistance, be finally delivered.

May the tax suggested by Nobel Prize laureate James Tobin be imposed in a reasonable and effective way on the current speculative operations that account for trillions of dollars traded every 24 hours. Then the United Nations, which cannot continue to depend on meager, inadequate and belated donations and charities, will have $1 trillion annually to save and develop the world. Given the seriousness and urgency of the existing problems, which have become a real hazard for the very survival of our species on the planet, this is what is actually needed, before it is too late.

Put an end to the ongoing genocide against the Palestinian people, which takes place while the world stares in amazement. May the basic right to life of that people, children and youth, be protected. May their right to peace and independence be respected; then, there will be nothing to fear from UN documents [emerging from the conference].

I am aware that the need for some relief from the awful situation their countries are facing, has led many friends from Africa and other regions to suggest the need for such prudence as would allow something to come out of this conference. I sympathize with them, but I cannot renounce my convictions, and I feel that the more candid we are in telling the truth, the more possibilities there will be to be respected and heeded. There have been enough centuries of deception.

I have only three short questions, based on realities that cannot be ignored. The capitalist, developed and wealthy countries today participate in an imperialist system born of capitalism itself and in an economic order that is imposed on the world, based on the philosophy of selfishness and brutal competition between men, nations and groups of nations, and which is completely indifferent to any feelings of solidarity or honest international cooperation. They live under the misleading, irresponsible and hallucinatory atmosphere of consumer societies. Regardless of the sincerity of their blind faith in such a system and the convictions of their most serious leaders, I wonder: Will they be able to understand the grave problems of today's world, which in its incoherent and uneven development, is ruled by blind laws, the huge power and the interests of the ever growing, increasingly uncontrollable and independent transnational corporations? Will they come to understand the impending universal chaos and rebellion? And, even if they wanted to, could they put an end to racism, racial discrimination, xenophobia and other related [forms of] intolerance, given that this is precisely what they represent?

From my viewpoint we are on the verge of a huge economic, social and political global crisis. Let us try to build an awareness about these realities, and alternatives will arise. History has shown that it is only from deep crises that great solutions have emerged. The peoples' right to life and justice will definitely assert itself in a thousand different shapes.

I believe in the mobilization and the struggle of the peoples! I believe in the idea of justice! I believe in truth! I believe in humanity!

14

"Thinking about the real or imagined parties involved in the bizarre holy war that is about to begin, I find it impossible to determine where the fanaticism is stronger."

The U.S. "War on Terrorism," Havana
September 22, 2001

No one can deny that terrorism constitutes today a dangerous and ethically indefensible phenomenon, that should be eradicated, in the face of its deep origins and the economic and political factors that brought it and those responsible for it to life.

The human and psychological damage brought on the people of the United States, the unexpected and shocking deaths of thousands of innocent people — whose images have shaken the world — have caused understandable and unanimous anger. But who has profited? The extreme right, the most backward and right-wing forces, those in favor of crushing a growing world rebellion and sweeping away everything progressive that still remains on the planet. Whoever organized or is responsible for such action committed an enormous error, a huge injustice and a great crime. But this tragedy should not be used to recklessly begin a war that in reality could unleash an endless carnage of people who are also innocent — in the name of justice and under the singular and bizarre title of "Infinite Justice" [later renamed "Operation Enduring Freedom"].

In the last few days we have witnessed the hasty establishment of the premise, the conception, the true purpose, the spirit and the conditions for such a war. No one could say that this was not something thought out well in advance, just waiting for its chance to materialize. After the so-called end of the Cold War, those who continued a military build-up and the development of the most sophisticated means to kill and exterminate human beings were aware that their large military investments would privilege them to impose absolute and complete dominance over other peoples of the world. The ideologues of the imperialist system knew very well what they were doing and why they were doing it.

Now, after the shock and sincere pain felt by all peoples on Earth for this atrocious and insane terrorist attack that targeted the U.S. people, the most extreme ideologues and the most belligerent hawks — already set in privileged positions of power — have taken command of the world's most powerful country, whose military and technological capabilities seem infinite. Its capacity to destroy and kill is enormous, while its inclination towards equanimity, serenity, thoughtfulness and restraint is minimal. A combination of elements — not discluding complicity by other rich and powerful countries who share a common enjoyment of similar privileges — prevailing opportunism, confusion and panic, make it almost impossible to avoid a bloody and unpredictable outcome.

The first victims of whatever military actions are undertaken will be the billions of people living in the poor and underdeveloped world. They already suffer unbelievable economic and social problems: unpayable debts and ruinous prices of their basic commodities; growing natural and ecological catastrophes; hunger and misery; massive undernourishment of their children, teenagers and adults; terrible AIDS epidemics; malaria; tuberculosis and infectious diseases that threaten whole nations with extermination.

The grave world economic crisis was already a real and irrefutable fact affecting absolutely every one of the big economic power centers. That crisis will under these new circumstances inevitably grow deeper and when it becomes unbearable for the overwhelming majority of people that crisis will bring chaos, rebellion and the impossibility of government.

The price would also be unpayable for rich countries. For years to come it could be impossible to speak strongly about the environment and ecology, about ideas or the results of research, or about projects for the protection of nature, because that space and opportunity would be taken for military actions, war, and crimes as infinite as "Infinite Justice," that is, the name pretending to denote the war operation yet to be unleashed.

Can there be any hope left, after listening, hardly 36 hours ago, to the speech made by the president before the U.S. Congress? I will avoid using adjectives, qualifiers or offensive words towards the author of that speech. They would be absolutely unnecessary, and untimely, when the tensions and seriousness of the moment advise thoughtfulness and equanimity. I will limit myself to underlining some short phrases that say it all:

"We will use every necessary weapon of war."

"Americans should not expect one battle, but a lengthy campaign unlike any other we have ever seen."

"Every nation in every region now has a decision to make. Either you are with us or you are with the terrorists."

"I've called the armed forces to alert and there is a reason. The hour is coming when America will act and you will make us proud."

"This is the world's fight, this is civilization's fight."

"I ask for your patience... in what will be a long struggle."

"The great achievements of our time and the great hopes of every time, now depend on us."

"The course of this conflict is not known, yet its outcome is certain... And we know that God is not neutral."

I ask every one of Cuba's citizens to meditate deeply and calmly on the ideas contained in several of the above-mentioned phrases.

"Either you are with us or you are with the terrorists." No nation of the world has been excluded from the dilemma, not even the big and powerful states; none has escaped the threat of war or attack.

"We will use any weapon." No procedure has been excluded, regardless of its ethical value, or any threat – however fatal – nuclear, chemical, biological or other.

"It will not be short combat but a lengthy war, lasting many years, unparalleled in history."

"It is the world's fight; it is civilization's fight."

"The achievements of our times and the hopes of every time, now depend on us."

Finally, a confession never before heard in a political speech made on the eve of war, no less than in times of apocalyptic risks: "The course of this conflict is not known; yet its outcome is certain. And we know that God is not neutral." This is an astonishing assertion. Thinking about the real or imagined parties involved in the bizarre holy war that is about to begin, I find it impossible to determine where the fanaticism is stronger.

On Thursday, before the U.S. Congress, the idea of a world military dictatorship was put forward, that would have the exclusive rule of force, irrespective of international laws or institutions. The United Nations, absolutely ignored in the present crisis, would fail to have any authority or prerogative whatsoever. There would be only one boss, only one judge, only one law.

All of us have been ordered to ally either with the U.S. Government, or with terrorism. Cuba, with the moral right that comes from being the country that has suffered the most and the longest from terrorist actions, the one whose people are not afraid of anything, because there is no threat or power in the world that can intimidate it, proclaims that it is opposed to terrorism, and opposed to war.

Although the possibilities of doing so are now remote, Cuba reaffirms the need to avert a war of unpredictable consequences, whose very authors have admitted to having not the least idea of how events will unfold. Likewise, Cuba reiterates its willingness to cooperate with all countries in the total eradication of terrorism.

An objective and calm friend should advise the U.S. Government against throwing young U.S. soldiers into an uncertain war in remote, isolated and inaccessible places, as if they were fighting against ghosts, not knowing where those ghosts are or even if they exist, or whether the people they kill are in fact responsible for the deaths of their innocent fellow citizens killed in the United States.

Cuba will never declare itself an enemy of the people of the United States. That people is today being subjected to an unprecedented [propaganda] campaign designed to sow hatred and a spirit of vengeance, so much so that even music that is meant to inspire peace has been banned. Instead, Cuba will make that music its own. Our children will sing songs for peace as long as the bloody war that has been announced continues.

Whatever happens, the territory of Cuba will never be used for terrorist actions against the U.S. people and we will do everything within our reach to prevent such actions against that people. Today we express our solidarity, and also urge peace and calmness. One day, they will admit we were right to do so.

If we are attacked, we will defend our independence, our principles and our social achievements with honor, to the last drop of blood! It will not be easy for them to fabricate pretexts to do it. Now, when they are talking about a war that would employ "all the necessary weapons," we would do well to recall that such an experience would not be a new one. Almost four decades ago, hundreds of strategic and tactical nuclear weapons were aimed at Cuba, yet not one of our compatriots lost sleep over that.

We are the children of that heroic people, and our patriotic and revolutionary conscience is more elevated than ever. It is the time for serenity and courage.

The world will grow aware of this and will raise its voice in the face of the terrible, threatening drama that it is about to suffer.

For Cubans, this is the precise moment to proclaim more proudly and resolutely than ever:

Homeland or Death!

Socialism or Death!

We will win!

15

"It would be better to build an enormous altar to peace where humankind can pay homage to all the innocent victims of blind terror and violence, be they U.S. or Afghan children."

On the Present Economic and World Crisis, Havana
November 2, 2001

In the mid-1990s, when globalization was extending around the planet, the United States achieved the most spectacular accumulation of wealth and power ever seen in history. As the absolute master of international financial institutions and through its immense political, military and technological strength, it was able to do so.

The world and capitalist society were entering an entirely new phase. Only an insignificant part of economic operations related to world production and trade. Every day, $3 trillion was involved in speculative operations such as currency and stock speculations. Stock prices on U.S. exchanges were rising like foam, often with no relation at all to the actual profits and revenues of companies. A number of myths were created: that there would never be another crisis and that the system could regulate itself. Capitalism had created the mechanisms it needed to advance and grow unimpeded. The creation of purely imaginary wealth reached such an extent that there were examples of stocks whose value increased 800 times in a period of only eight years. It was like an enormous balloon that supposedly could inflate toward infinity.

As this virtual wealth was created, it was also invested, spent and wasted. Historical experience was completely ignored. The world's population had quadrupled in only 100 years. There were billions of human beings who neither participated in nor enjoyed this wealth in any way whatsoever. They supplied raw materials and cheap labor, but did not consume and could not be consumers. They did not constitute a market. They were not part of that immense sea fed by the almost infinite river of products flowing, in the midst of fierce competition, from ever more productive factories that created ever fewer jobs, based in a privileged and highly limited group of industrialized countries.

An elementary analysis was sufficient to comprehend that this situation was unsustainable. Nobody seemed to realize that apparently insignificant occurrences in the economy of one region of the world could shake the entire structure of the world economy.

The architects, specialists and administrators of the new international economic order — economists and politicians — now look on as their fantasy falls to pieces, yet they barely understand that they have lost control of events. Other forces are in control: on the one hand, those of the large, increasingly powerful and independent transnationals and, on the other, the stubborn realities that are waiting for the world to truly change.

In July 1997, the first major crisis of the globalized neoliberal world erupted. The tigers fell to pieces. Japan still has not managed to recover, and the world continues to suffer the consequences.

In August 1998 came the so-called Russian crisis. Despite this country's insignificant contribution to the worldwide GDP — barely 2% — the U.S. stock markets were badly shaken, dropping by hundreds of points in a matter of hours.

In January 1999, only five months later, the Brazilian crisis broke out. An all-out joint effort by the G-7, the IMF and the World Bank was needed to prevent the crisis from spreading throughout South America and dealing a devastating blow to the U.S. stock markets...

There are people who calmly speak today about the "world economic crisis caused by the terrorist attacks that took place in the United States on September 11, and by the war against Afghanistan initiated on October 7." Such statements are completely baseless. What I have just outlined irrefutably proves this. The crisis was already breaking out, uncontrollably...

The economic crisis is not a consequence of the September 11 attacks and the war against Afghanistan. Such claims could only be made out of total ignorance or in an attempt to hide the real causes. The crisis is a consequence of the resounding and irreversible failure of an economic and political conception imposed on the world: neoliberalism and neoliberal globalization.

The terrorist attacks and the war did not give rise to the crisis, but they have considerably aggravated it. What had been rapidly advancing was abruptly boosted even further. Humanity must now confront three extremely serious problems, all of which feed off one another: terrorism, war and the economic crisis.

The economic crisis also means the aggravation of major problems that are far from being solved: poverty, hunger and disease, which kill tens of millions of people in the world every year; illiteracy; lack of education; unemployment; the exploitation of millions of children through child labor and prostitution; the trafficking and consumption of drugs, which mobilizes and absorbs hundreds of billions of dollars; money laundering; the lack of drinking water and the scarcity of housing, hospitals, communications, schools and educational facilities. Fundamental rights of all human beings are affected.

The crisis will have an especially negative impact on the struggle for sustainable development; the preservation of the environment and the protection of nature from the merciless destruction it is being subjected to and which is causing the poisoning of water and the atmosphere; the destruction of the ozone layer; deforestation; desertification and the extinction of animals and plants. How could these issues not be taken into the slightest account?

There are nations and even entire regions in some continents that could be annihilated if terrifying plagues like AIDS are not urgently combated and defeated by humankind, and if terrorism, war and the economic crisis are not resolutely confronted. Now is the time, more than ever before, when cooperation among all countries is needed...

Although we have made our stance known, I think it is worthwhile to recall that on September 11, just hours after the events, having expressed our total condemnation of the brutal attacks and our sincere and selfless solidarity with the U.S. people — since we never asked for or expected anything in return — we expressed a conviction that we continue to hold today, with more strength and certainty than ever: "None of the present problems of the world can be solved by force... The international community should build a world consciousness against terrorism... Only the intelligent policy of seeking strength through consensus and international public opinion can decidedly uproot this problem... This unimaginable event should serve to launch an international struggle against terrorism... The world cannot be saved unless a path of international peace and cooperation is pursued."

A week later, on September 22, I declared on behalf of our people: "Whatever happens — that is to say, whether or not there is a war — the territory of Cuba will never be used for terrorist actions against the U.S. people."

I added something else: "We will do everything within our reach to prevent such actions against that people. Today we express our solidarity, and also urge peace and calmness. One day, they will admit we were right to do so."

On September 29, at a rally held in Ciego de Avila, I continued to stress our point of view: "No one should be misled into thinking that the peoples of the world, including a number of honest political leaders, will not react when the war becomes a reality and its horrific images start to be seen. Such images will then take the place of the sad and shocking images of the events in New York, at a time when forgetting them would cause irreparable damage to the spirit of solidarity with the U.S. people. That solidarity is today a fundamental element in the eradication of terrorism, without needing to resort to a war of unpredictable consequences and avoiding the death of an incalculable number of innocents.

"The first victims can already be seen. They are the millions trying to escape the war and the dying children with ghostly appearances whose images will disturb the world. No one could prevent the dissemination of these images."

The events that have been taking place make it increasingly clear how right we were. An editorial in *Granma*, the official newspaper of Cuba's Communist Party, published on October 8, just hours after the war had been unleashed, stated: "This is not a war against terrorism... it is a war in favor of terrorism, since the military operations will make it more complicated and difficult to eradicate terrorism. War is like pouring oil on the flames.

"From now on, there will be a great avalanche of news about bombs, missiles, air strikes, the advance of armored vehicles; troops of ethnic groups allied with the invaders; the dropping of paratroopers or the ground advance of the elite forces of the attacking countries. Soon, there will be news about occupied cities, including the capital, and TV images of whatever the censors permit or that escapes control. The war will be against the people of that country [Afghanistan] and not against the terrorists. There are no battalions or armies of terrorists. That is a dark concept and a sinister method of struggling against ghosts."

After 26 days of relentless bombing, those who have been following events day by day can see that what has happened up until now is exactly as we predicted.

The war began inexorably. We knew that it was extremely unlikely, practically impossible, that it would not happen. This has not led us, however, either before or after, to become discouraged or to renounce our stance.

We insisted that it was necessary to fight against terrorism and against the war. We were never led by a spirit of revenge or hatred against the United States. It was with sadness that I meditated on the mistake that, in my view, was being made but I never uttered an insult or a personal offense. I have often said to those involved in this battle of ideas that there is never a need to personally offend anyone. I would rather enumerate facts, avoid adjectives, analyze with a cool head and in this way wage arguments. Doing so preserves our moral authority and prevents anyone from questioning the strength and sincerity of our position.

Presently, I am afraid that if the possibility existed to defeat terrorism without a war, through cooperation and with the unanimous support of the entire international community — leading to truly efficient measures and to the building of a strong moral conscience against terrorism — that possibility tends to fade with every passing day.

The worst would be to reach a point when it is no longer possible to find such a solution, because I see it ever more clearly that it is absurd and impossible to try to resolve this through war. I have tried to imagine what was going through the minds of the U.S. political and military strategists — maybe they thought that a colossal deployment of forces would crush the will of the Taliban, perhaps they were hopeful that an initial and devastating blow would attain that objective.

Everybody knows the estimates made by NATO during the war against Yugoslavia. The idea then was that NATO's objectives would be accomplished in five days but almost 80 days passed and still it had not happened. It is also known that at the end of 80 days, despite an extraordinary display of technology and power, the Serbian army was practically intact. When the time came to fight on the ground, something that the members of the coalition were not particularly fond of, the envoys of Russia and Finland had to use their weight heavily to "persuade" the adversary [to withdraw] through diplomatic channels.

I do not share the view that the main pursuit of the United States in Afghanistan was oil. I rather see it as part of its geo-strategic design. No one would commit such a mistake simply in pursuit of oil, least of all a country with access to all the oil in the world, including all the Russian oil and gas it desires. It would be sufficient for the U.S. to invest in, buy and pay for oil. Based on its privileges, the United States can even purchase oil by minting reserve bonds on a 30 year maturity span. That is how, over more than 80 years, it has bought products and services accounting for over $6.6 trillion.

Military actions in Afghanistan are fraught with dangers. It is an extremely troubled area where two large countries [Pakistan and India] have fought several wars. There are profound national and religious antagonisms between them. The population of the disputed territory is mostly Islamic. As tempers grow frail, a war might break out, and both countries have nuclear capabilities. The destabilization of the Pakistani Government by the war is a serious risk. That government is placed in a highly complicated position. The Taliban emerged there, and they share the same Pashtun ethnic background with an undetermined number of Pakistanis — no less than 10 million is the most conservative figure among those that have been mentioned. They also share with fanatic passion the same religious beliefs.

The U.S. military are usually well versed in their trade. I have met some of them when, after retiring, they have visited Cuba as scholars. They write books, tell stories and make their political analyses. I was therefore not surprised by information released in *The New Yorker* magazine of October 29 that described a contingency plan to seize the Pakistani nuclear warheads, in case a radical group took over the government of that country. It was absolutely impossible for U.S. strategists to overlook such a substantial risk. Yet every bomb dropped on Afghanistan, every picture of dead children or people dying or suffering terrible wounds, compounds that risk. What is hard to imagine is how those responsible for protecting [the nuclear weapons] will react to a plan that is by now in the public domain as much as is *Chronicle of a Death Foretold* by Gabriel García Márquez.

I am personally not aware of something the U.S. intelligence agencies should know only too well — that is, where and how those nuclear warheads are kept and the way in which they are protected. I try to imagine, and it is not easy, how such an action could be conducted by elite troops. One day, perhaps, someone might tell how it could be done. I find it harder still to imagine the political scenario in the aftermath of such an action when the fight would then be against an additional 100 million Muslims. The U.S. Government has denied the existence of such a contingency plan. This was to be expected. It could not have done otherwise.

The most logical question I have is whether the heads of government and the leaders, who are friends of the United States and who have longstanding political and practical experience, foresaw these potential dangers? If they did, why did they not warn the United States and try to dissuade it? Obviously, the friends of the United States fear such danger but do not fully appreciate it.

It is always difficult to try to guess when it comes to these issues. There is something, however, of which I am absolutely certain: if 20,000 or 30,000 men used clever methods of irregular warfare, the same number that the United States itself wants to deploy there, then that struggle could last 20 years. It is completely impossible to subdue the Afghan adversary in an irregular warfare on that country's ground with bombs and missiles, whatever the caliber and the power of those weapons. The Afghans have already been through the hardest of psychological moments. They have lost everything:

family, housing and property. They have absolutely nothing else they can lose. Nothing seems to indicate that they will surrender their weapons, even if their most notable leaders are killed.

I am simply expressing my thoughts to you. I think the best way to show solidarity with the U.S. people — who lost thousands of innocent lives in the outrageous attack, including those of children, young people and old people, men and women — is by frankly speaking our minds. The sacrifice of those lives should not be in vain, but rather should be used to save many other lives, to prove that thinking and conscience can be stronger than terror and death.

We are not suggesting that crimes committed on Earth should be left unpunished. I do not have the elements of judgment to accuse anyone in particular, but if the culprits were those that the U.S. Government is punishing and trying to remove, there is no doubt that the way in which they are doing it will lead to the creation of altars where the alleged murderers will be worshiped as saints by millions of men and women.

It would be better to build an enormous altar to peace where humankind can pay homage to all the innocent victims of blind terror and violence, be they U.S. or Afghan children. I say this as someone who considers himself an adversary of U.S. policies but not an enemy of that people, and as one who believes he has some idea of human history, psychology and justice.

FIDEL CASTRO READER

The voice of one of the 20th century's most controversial political figures — as well as one of the world's greatest orators — is captured in this new selection of Castro's key speeches over 40 years.
ISBN 1-876175-11-7

CHE GUEVARA READER
Writings on Guerrilla Strategy, Politics and Revolution
Edited by David Deutschmann
The most complete selection of Guevara's writings, letters and speeches available in English. An unprecedented source of primary material on Cuba and Latin America in the 1950s and 1960s.
ISBN 1-875284-93-1

CUBAN REVOLUTION READER
A Documentary History
Edited by Julio García Luis
This Reader documents the development of the Cuban Revolution, one of the defining events of the 20th century, highlighting 40 key episodes over the past four decades.
ISBN 1-876175-10-9 *Also available in Spanish (ISBN 1-876175-28-1)*

JOSE MARTI READER
Writings on the Americas
An outstanding new anthology of the writings, letters and poetry of one of the most important and brilliant Latin American voices of the 19th century.
ISBN 1-875284-12-5

SALVADOR ALLENDE READER
Chile's Voice of Democracy
Edited by James D. Cockcroft and Jane Carolina Canning
This new book makes available for the first time in English Allende's voice and vision of a more democratic, peaceful and just world.
ISBN 1-876175-24-9

MY EARLY YEARS
By Fidel Castro
Fidel Castro reflects on his childhood, youth and student days in an unprecedented and remarkably candid manner. Introductory essay by Gabriel García Márquez
ISBN 1-876175-07-9

CHE — A MEMOIR BY FIDEL CASTRO
For the first time Fidel Castro writes with candor and affection of his relationship with Ernesto Che Guevara, documenting his extraordinary bond with Cuba.
ISBN 1-875284-15-X

I WAS NEVER ALONE
A Prison Diary from El Salvador
By Nidia Díaz
Nidia Díaz gives a dramatic and inspiring personal account of her experience as a guerrilla commander during El Salvador's civil war. Seriously wounded, she was captured in combat by Cuban-exile CIA agent Félix Rodríguez.
ISBN 1-876175-17-6

INSIDE APARTHEID'S PRISON
Notes and Letters of Struggle
By Raymond Suttner
"Raymond Suttner is one of a small number of white comrades who played a substantial role in bring apartheid to an end. His book should be read by all who are interested in South Africa." Walter Sisulu
ISBN 1-876175-25-7

SLOVO
The Unfinished Autobiography of ANC Leader Joe Slovo
A revealing and highly entertaining autobiography of one of the key figures of South Africa's African National Congress. Introduction by Nelson Mandela.
ISBN 1-875284-95-8

AFROCUBA
An Anthology of Cuban Writing on Race, Politics and Culture
Edited by Pedro Pérez Sarduy and Jean Stubbs
What is it like to be Black in Cuba? Does racism exist in a revolutionary society that claims to have abolished it? *AfroCuba* looks at the Black experience through the eyes of the island's writers, scholars and artists.
ISBN 1-875284-41-9

CUBA AND THE UNITED STATES
A Chronological History
By Jane Franklin
This chronology relates in detail the developments involving the two neighboring countries from the 1959 revolution through 1995.
ISBN 1-875284-92-3

CUBA — TALKING ABOUT REVOLUTION
Conversations with Juan Antonio Blanco by Medea Benjamin
One of Cuba's outstanding intellectuals discusses Cuba today, featuring an essay, "Cuba: 'socialist museum' or social laboratory?"
ISBN 1-875284-97-4

IN THE SPIRIT OF WANDERING TEACHERS
The Cuban Literacy Campaign, 1961
A graphic record capturing the youthful spirit of the early years of the Cuban revolution. Text in English and Spanish. Photos.
ISBN 1-876175-39-7

HAVANA–MIAMI
The U.S.–Cuba migration conflict
By Jesús Arboleya
This book examines the origins of the migration conflict and why it has become such an important U.S. domestic issue.
ISBN 1-875284-91-5

CAPITALISM IN CRISIS
Globalization and World Politics Today
By Fidel Castro

Cuba's leader adds his voice to the growing international chorus against neoliberalism and globalization. In this substantial collection, Fidel Castro also analyzes:

- U.S. "war on drugs" in Latin America
- Need to democratize the United Nations
- Danger of a new stock market collapse

ISBN 1-876175-18-4

VIOLENCE AND TERROR IN LATIN AMERICA
A Century of Crimes Against Humanity
By Luis Suárez

An outstanding new examination of crimes against humanity perpetrated on the peoples of Latin America and the Carribbean.

ISBN 1-876175-41-9

GLOBAL JUSTICE
Liberation and Socialism
By Ernesto Che Guevara

Is there an alternative to the neoliberal globalization that is ravaging our planet? Collected here are three classic works by Che Guevara.

ISBN 1-876175-45-1

LATIN AMERICA: FROM COLONIZATION TO GLOBALIZATION
Noam Chomsky in conversation with Heinz Dieterich

An indispensable book for those interested in Latin America and the politics and history of the region.

ISBN 1-876175-13-3

Ocean Press
Australia: GPO Box 3279, Melbourne 3001, Australia
      • Fax: 61-3-9329 5040
USA: PO Box 1186, Old Chelsea Stn., New York, NY 10113-1186
      • Tel: 1-718-246 4160

E-mail: info@oceanbooks.com.au
www.oceanbooks.com.au